The Ottawa Car Company

TROLLEY CAR,
ELECTRIC LOCOMOTIVE
AND
MOTOR BUS CATALOG

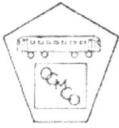

Ottawa Car Manufacturing Co.,
LIMITED

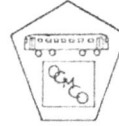

OTTAWA, CANADA

ISBN #978-1-935700-10-4

PRESIDENT   -   T. AHEARN

VICE-PRESIDENT & GENERAL MANAGER
W. H. McINTYRE

DIRECTORS

T. F. AHEARN	G. F. HENDERSON, K.C.
E. N. SOPER	COL. G. P. MURPHY, C.M.G.
C. MacNAB	K. FELLOWES

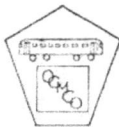

Ottawa Car Manufacturing Co.,
LIMITED
OTTAWA, CANADA

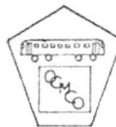

I N submitting this catalogue we are placing before you a list of articles, manufactured by us, in Canada, for which there is an ever-increasing demand.

We have endeavoured to illustrate and describe as fully and as clearly as possible each article in detail.

The description and illustration of all products we have manufactured in the past, or are capable of manufacturing, would be too voluminous for a practical catalogue.

Unlimited resources, unsurpassed plant equipment and capacity, our extended experience and resultant skill, assure a quality product, right prices and up-to-the-minute service.

In order to give our customers the best possible service, we make it a very important duty in our Shipping Department to forward goods which are standard and in stock the same day that the order arrives at our office, unless the order specifies otherwise. We, therefore, carry at all times a large quantity of each article which we consider through past experience, a standard article, required for maintenance, to give service to our customers.

We respectfully solicit your business and in return we guarantee satisfaction and service.

We have forwarded this catalogue personally as we require these catalogues to be identified by their ownership and a record of it has been made by us so that additional or revised pages may be sent to you from time to time.

Faithfully yours,

OTTAWA CAR MANUFACTURING COMPANY LIMITED,
OTTAWA, ONTARIO.

SERIAL No..................

In the event of transfer please advise, so that we may change our records accordingly.

INDEX

INDEX CONTINUED

CAR AND BUS FITTINGS—Continued.

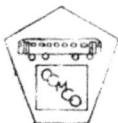

INDEX CONTINUED

CAR AND BUS FITTINGS—Continued.

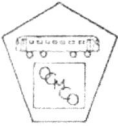 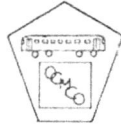

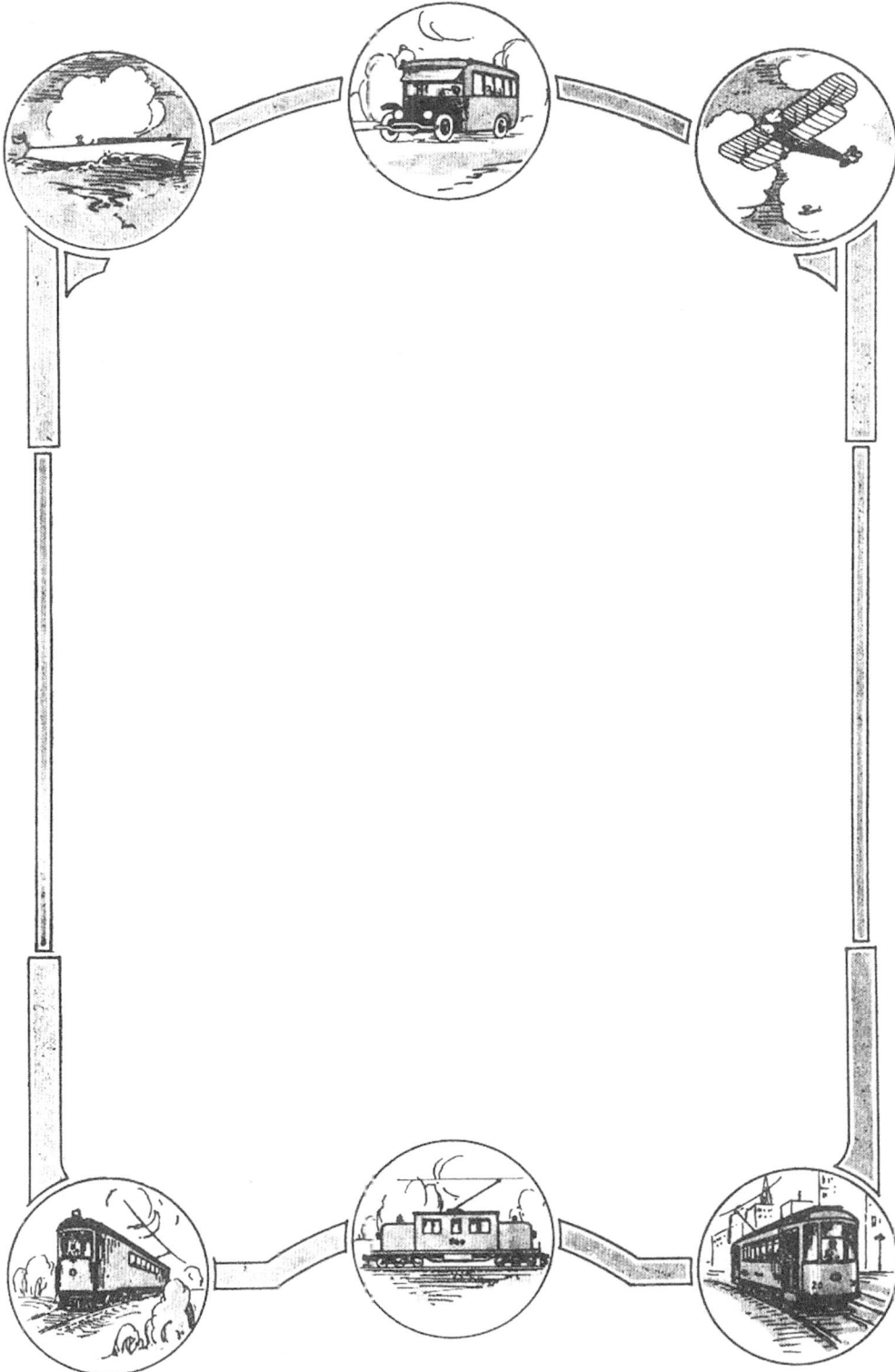

Dimensions

Length over Anti-Climbers.................51' 2"
Truck Centres...........................26' 6"
Wheel base...............................6' 6"
Width of Seat...........................37½"
Rail to Step.............................16"
Step to Platform........................14⅛"
Seating Capacity.........................50
Width of Aisle...........................18"
Diameter of Wheels.......................33"

Weights and Equipment

Car body..............................31,460 lbs.
Motors and Equipment..................16,800 lbs.
Trucks................................18,240 lbs.
    TOTAL...........66,500 lbs.
Motors and type.......Four. WEST. 548-C-2
H.P. per Motor.........................100
Gear Ratio...........................24-65
Control...........................WEST. H.L.
Air Brakes........................WEST. AMM.

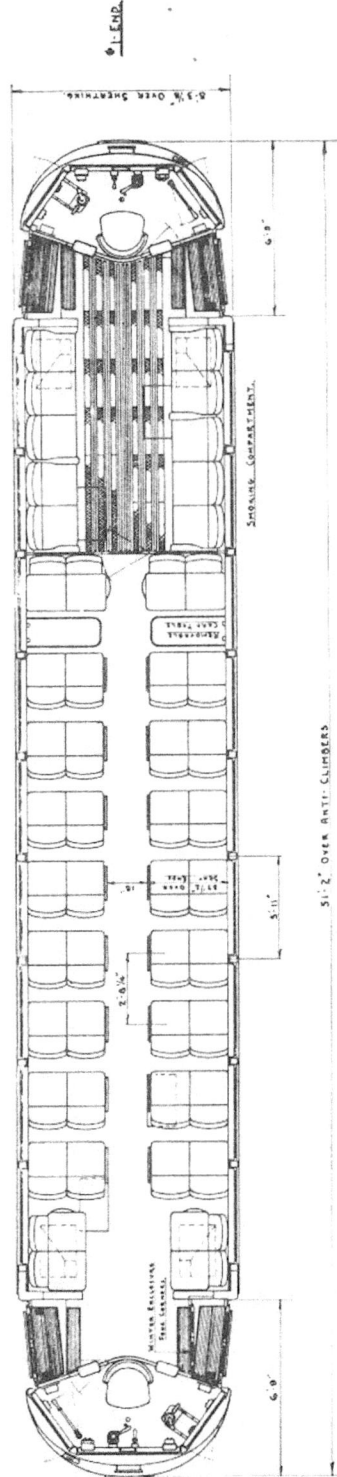

**50 Passenger, Double Truck, Double End, Interurban
Motor Car for HYDRO ELECTRIC RAILWAYS**

50 Passenger, Double Truck, Double End, Interurban Motor Car for HYDRO ELECTRIC RAILWAYS

Dimensions

Length over Anti-Climbers	51'2"
Truck Centres	26'6"
Wheel base	6'6"
Width of Seat	37½"
Rail to Step	16"
Step to Platform	14⅛"
Seating Capacity	50
Width of Aisle	18"
Diameter of Wheels	33"

Weights and Equipment

Car body	26,860 lbs.
Equipment	900 lbs.
Trucks	18,240 lbs.
TOTAL	46,000 lbs.
Control	WEST. H.L.
Air Brakes	WEST. ATM.

50 Passenger, Double Truck, Double End, Interurban

Trailer Car, for HYDRO ELECTRIC RAILWAYS

50 Passenger, Double Truck, Double End, Interurban
Trailer Car, for HYDRO ELECTRIC RAILWAYS

Dimensions

Length over Bumpers	45' 11⅞"
Truck centres	21' 2"
Wheel base	5' 4"
Width of seat	34"
Rail to Step	12¾"
Step to Platform	13¼"
Seating Capacity	51
Width of Aisle	24¾"
Diameter of Wheels	26"

Weights and Equipment

Car body	18,400 lbs.
Motors and Equipment	10,350 lbs.
Trucks	12,200 lbs.
TOTAL	40,950 lbs.
Motors and type	Four, C.G.E.-247J
H.P. per motor	40
Gear Ratio	15-58
Control	K-35
Air Brakes	WEST. Safety Control

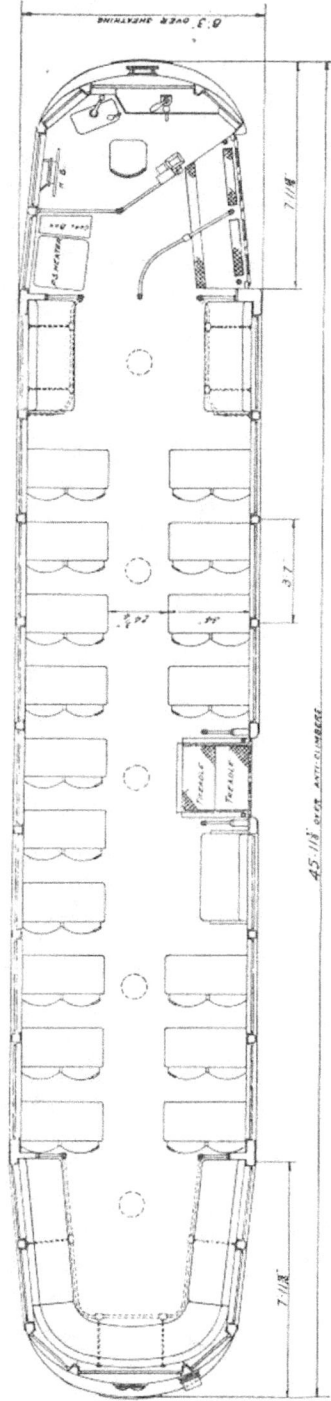

51 Passenger, Double Truck, Single End, Pay Enter, Center Exit,
Safety Car, EDMONTON RADIAL RAILWAY

51 Passenger, Double Truck, Single End, Pay Enter, Center Exit, Safety Car, EDMONTON RADIAL RAILWAY

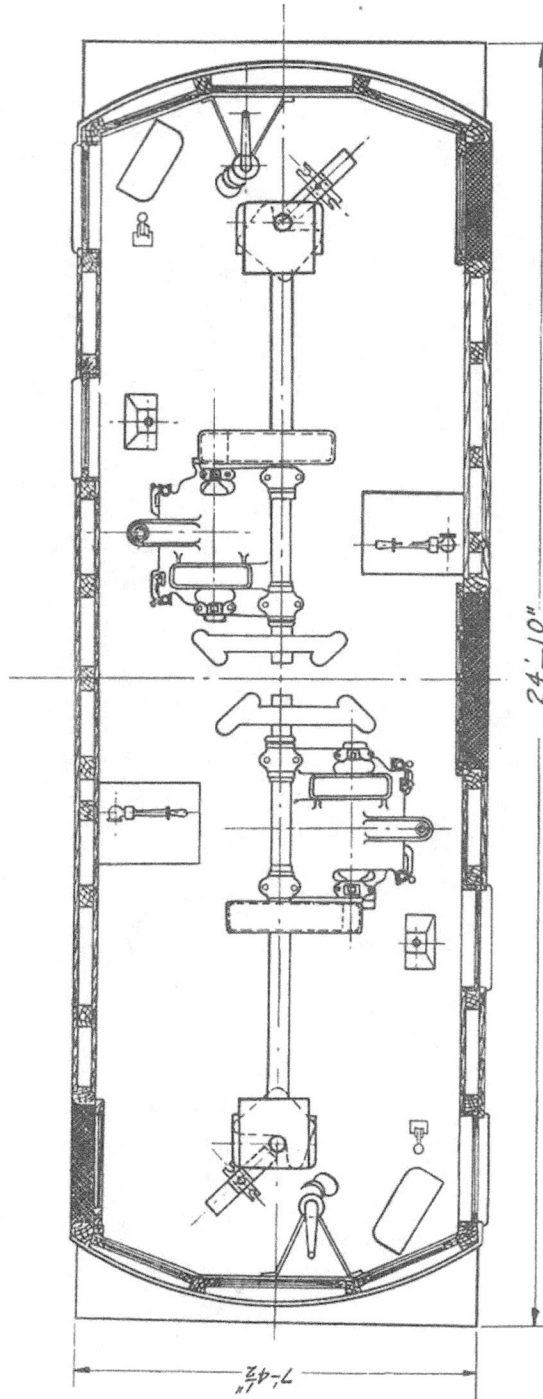

SINGLE TRUCK BEVEL GEAR-DRIVE SNOW SWEEPER

MONTREAL TRAMWAYS

Dimensions

Length over devil strip leveler 33' 4"
Length of underframe...... 24' 11"
Wheel base................ 7' 0"
Rail to floor.............. 4' 8"
Diameter of wheels........ 33"

Weights and Equipment

Total weight.......... 22,000 lbs.

SINGLE TRUCK, BEVEL GEAR DRIVE, SNOW SWEEPER

Dimensions

Length overall..........	39' 6"
Truck centres..........	12' 6"
Wheel base.............	4' 6"
Rail to floor...........	4' 5"
Diameter of wheels.....	33"

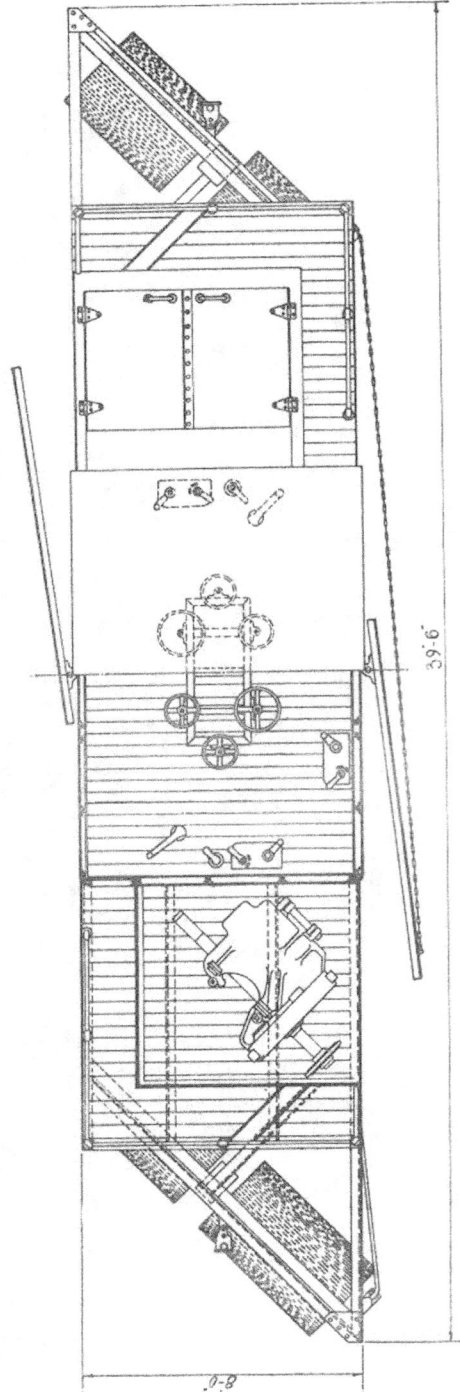

Weights and Equipment

Total...............	52,000 lbs.
Motors and type—4 motors, West.	
No. 101-B.	
H.P. per motor—45 H.P.	
Gear ratio—15-69.	
Control—K.	

COMBINATION LOCOMOTIVE AND SWEEPER

COMBINATION LOCOMOTIVE AND SWEEPER

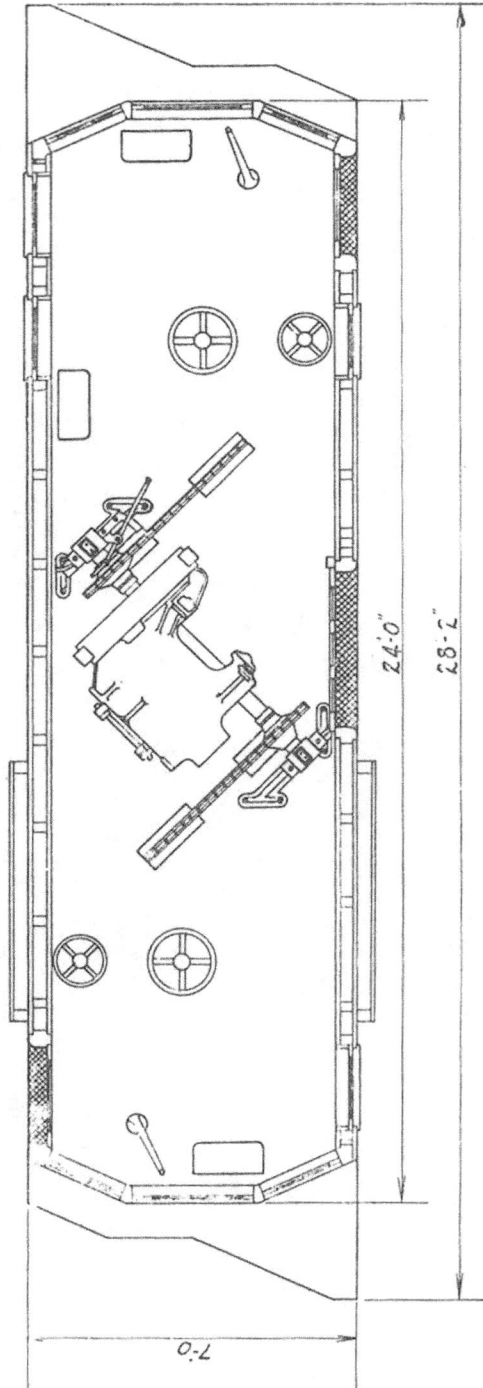

COMBINATION SNOW SWEEPER & TOWER CAR

Dimensions

Length over bumpers........ 28' 2"
Wheel base................. 7' 0"
Rail to floor.............. 4' 5"
Diameter of wheels......... 33"

Weights and Equipment

Total weight ....23,600 lbs.

COMBINATION SNOW PLOW SWEEPER
AND TOWER CAR

Dimensions

Length over bumpers	32' 0"
Truck centres	18' 0"
Wheel base	6' 6"
Rail to floor	4' 4"
Diameter of wheels	36"

Weights and Equipment

Body and equipment	64,000 lbs.
Trucks and motors	36,000 lbs.
Total	100,000 lbs.

Motors and type—4 motors—West. 562-D.5.

Type interpole 600 volts.

H.P. per motor—100 H.P.

Gear ratio—17-60

Control—West. H.L.F. double end control.

50 TON LOCOMOTIVE

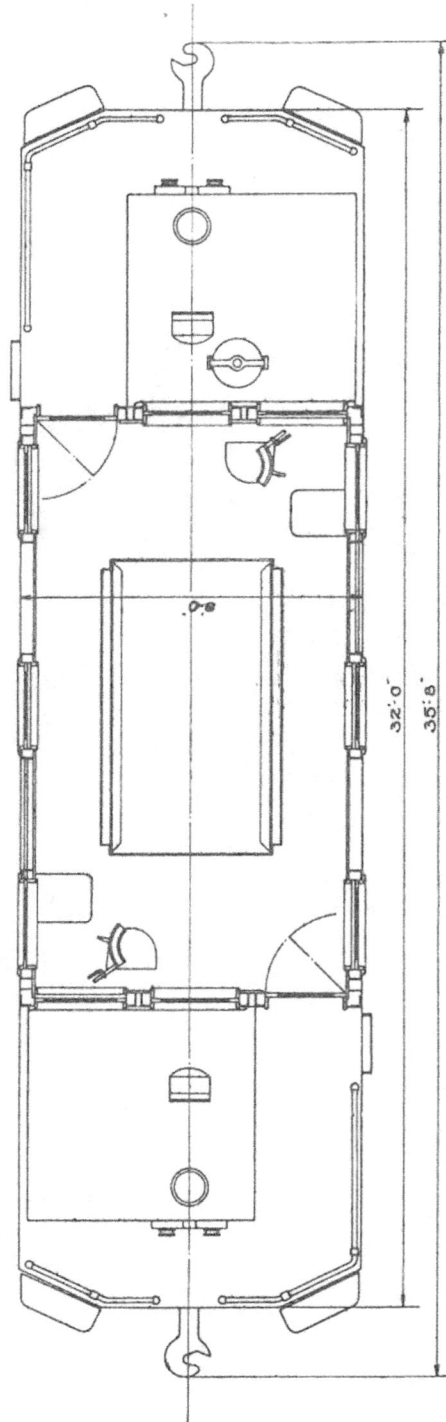

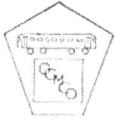

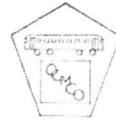

50 TON LOCOMOTIVE

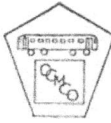

Dimensions

Length overall............	45′ 3¾″
Truck centres............	20′ 0″
Wheel base..............	5′ 2″
Width of seat...........	32½″
Rail to step.............	15⅜″
Step to platform.........	12″
Seating capacity.........	44
Width of aisle...........	20⅝″
Diameter of wheels.......	26″

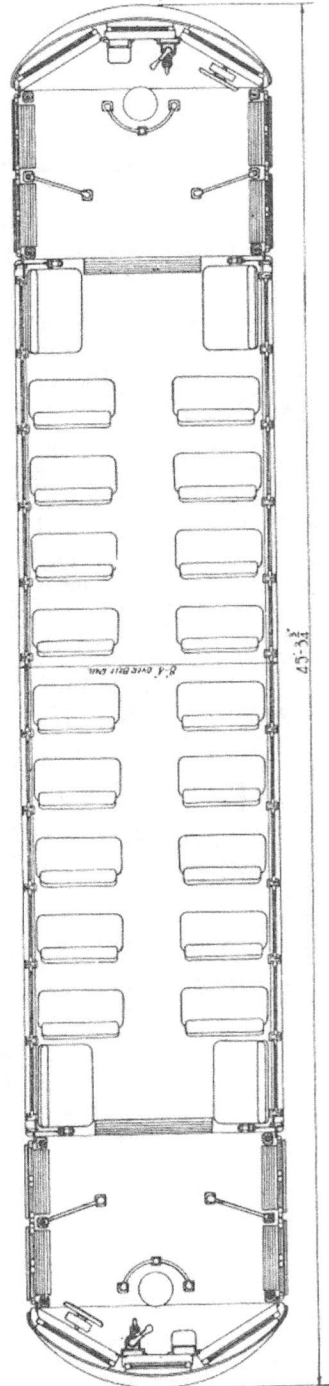

Weights and Equipment

Car body and equipment	23,200 lbs.
Trucks and motors......	16,800 lbs.
Total..........	40,000 lbs.
Motors and type—G.E. 256.	
H.P. per motor—35.	
Control—H.L. (West.)	

44 PASSENGER DOUBLE END—DOUBLE TRUCK SAFETY CAR

HYDRO ELECTRIC RAILWAY, WINDSOR.

44 PASSENGER, DOUBLE END, DOUBLE TRUCK, SAFETY CAR

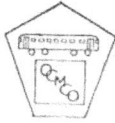

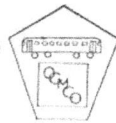

Dimensions

Length over bumpers	30' 9¼"
Wheel base	8'0"
Width of seat—longitudinal seats.	
Rail to step	15"
Step to platform	14¼"
Seating capacity	30
Diameter of wheels	26"

Weights and equipment

Car body and equipment	8,240 lbs.
Trucks and motors	7,260 lbs.
Total	15,500 lbs.

Motors and type—2 motors, West. 508-A.

H.P. per motor—25.

Gear ratio—13-74

Control—K.

7'-8" OVER SHEETING

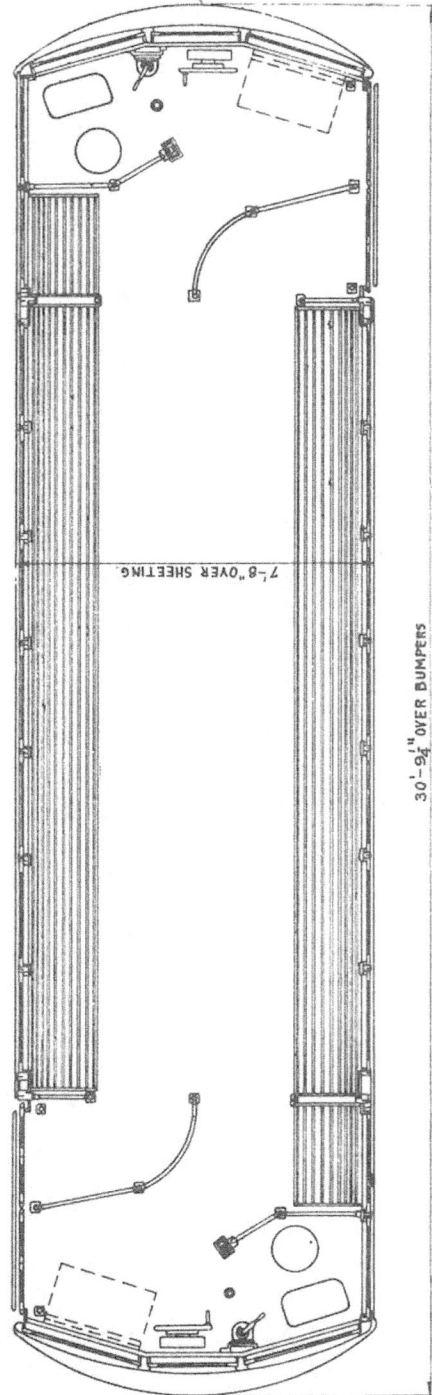

30'-9¼" OVER BUMPERS

30 PASSENGER SINGLE TRUCK DOUBLE END SAFETY CAR

Kitchener Railway

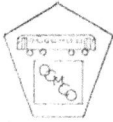

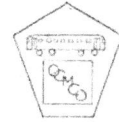

30 PASSENGER SINGLE TRUCK, DOUBLE END, SAFETY CAR

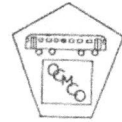

Dimensions

Length over bumpers	45′ 3¾″
Truck centres	20′-0″
Wheel base	5′ 4″
Width of seat	34″
Rail to step	13⅞″
Step to platform	13½″
Seating capacity	52
Width of aisle	25½″—1219
	28⅜″—1225
Diameter of wheels	26″

Weights and Equipment

Car body and equipment	20,250 lbs.
Trucks and motors	18,500 lbs.
Total	38,750 lbs.
Motors and type—4 West. 510-A-2.	
H.P. per motor—42.	
Gear ratio—13-69.	
Control—K.	

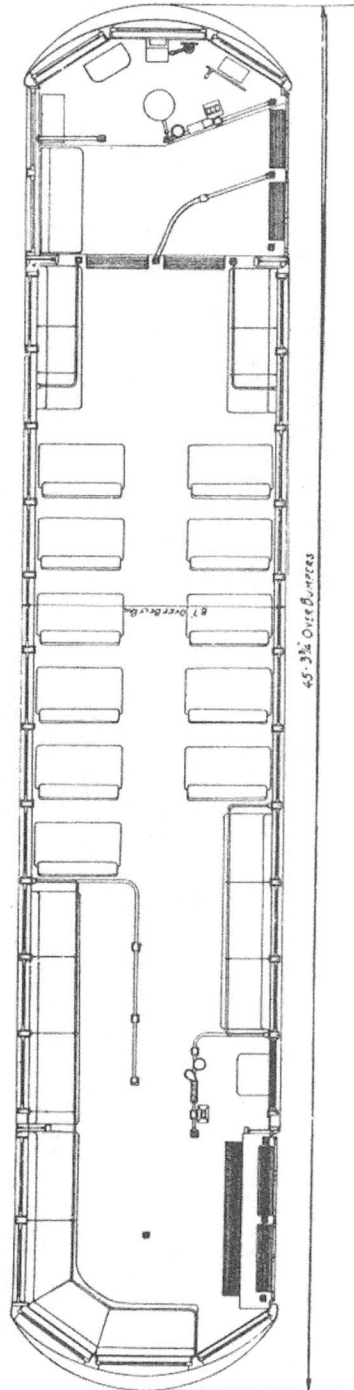

52 PASSENGER PAY-AS-YOU-LEAVE SAFETY CAR

OTTAWA ELECTRIC RAILWAY

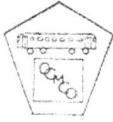

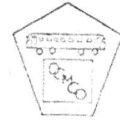

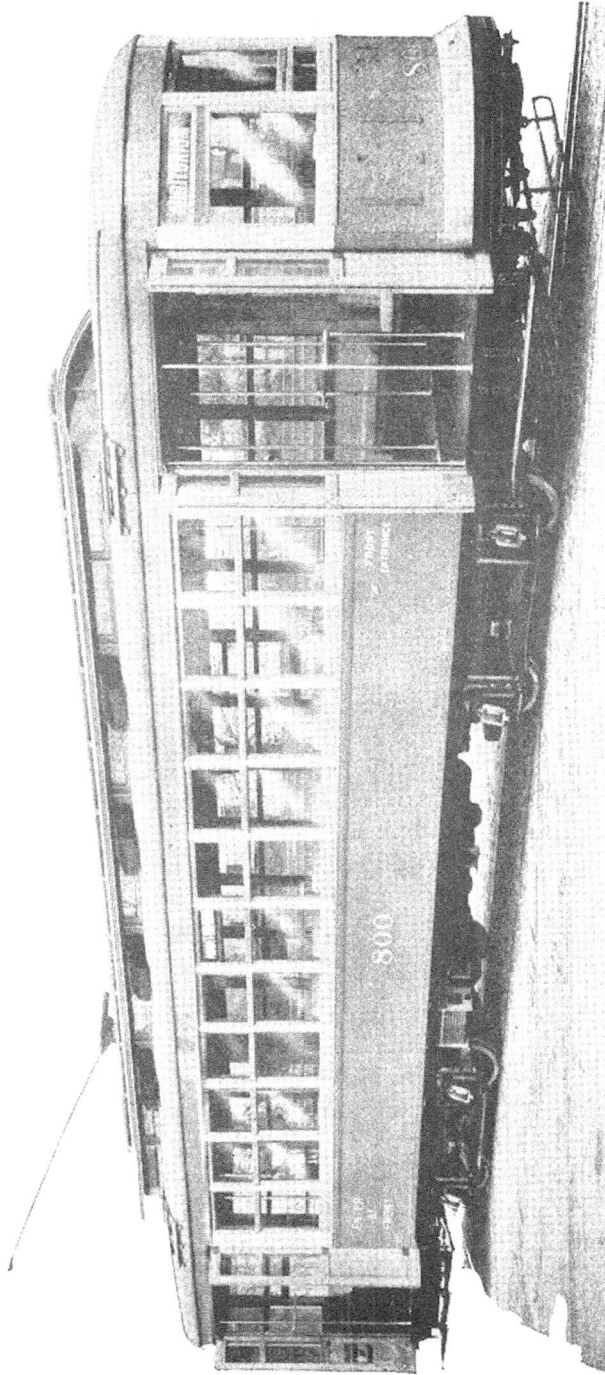

52 PASSENGER PAY-AS-YOU-LEAVE CAR.

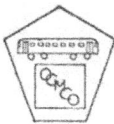

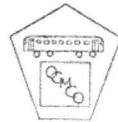

Weights and Equipment

Car body and equipment 31,600 lbs.
Trucks and motors...... 24,700 lbs.
Total......... 56,300 lbs.
Motors and type—4 G.E. 217 B.
H.P. per motor—50.
Control—K-35 H.H. control.

Dimensions

Length over bumpers...... 50′ 2¾″
Truck centres............. 27′ 6″
Wheel base............... 6′ 0″
Width of seat............ 33″
Rail to step............. 15″
Step to platform—14½″ & 1 step 11½″
Seating capacity......... 52
Width of aisle........... 20¾″
Diameter of wheels....... 33″

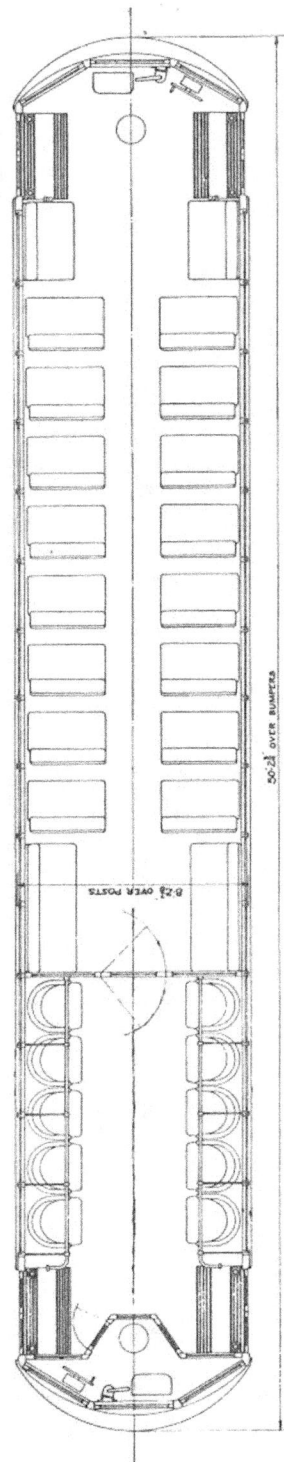

52 PASSENGER—END ENTRANCE INTERURBAN CAR

HYDRO ELECTRIC RAILWAY

52 PASSENGER—END ENTRANCE—INTERURBAN CAR

Dimensions

Length over bumpers	27' 9½"
Wheel base	8' 0"
Width of seat	31¼"
Rail to step	15⅝"
Step to platform	14½"
Seating capacity	32
Width of aisle	21"
Diameter of wheels	26"

Weights and Equipment

Car body and equipment	12,110 lbs.
Trucks and motors	6,390 lbs.
Total	18,500 lbs.
Motors and type	2-G.E. 258-C.
H.P. per motor	25 H.P.
Control	K-63 controllers

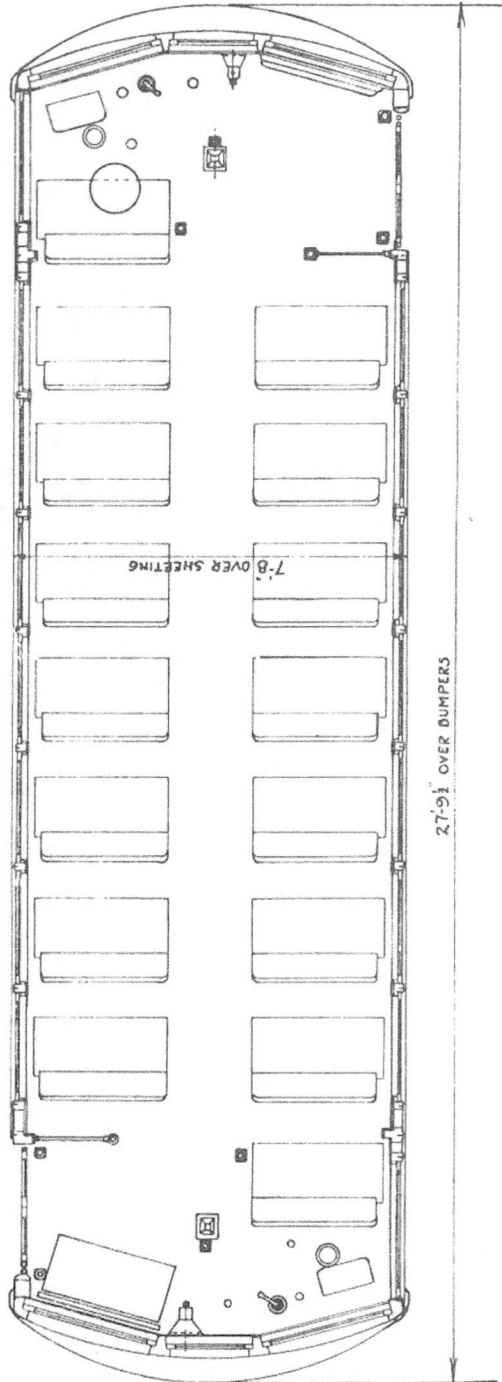

7'-8 OVER SHEETING

27'-9½" OVER BUMPERS

32 PASSENGER—SINGLE TRUCK SAFETY CAR

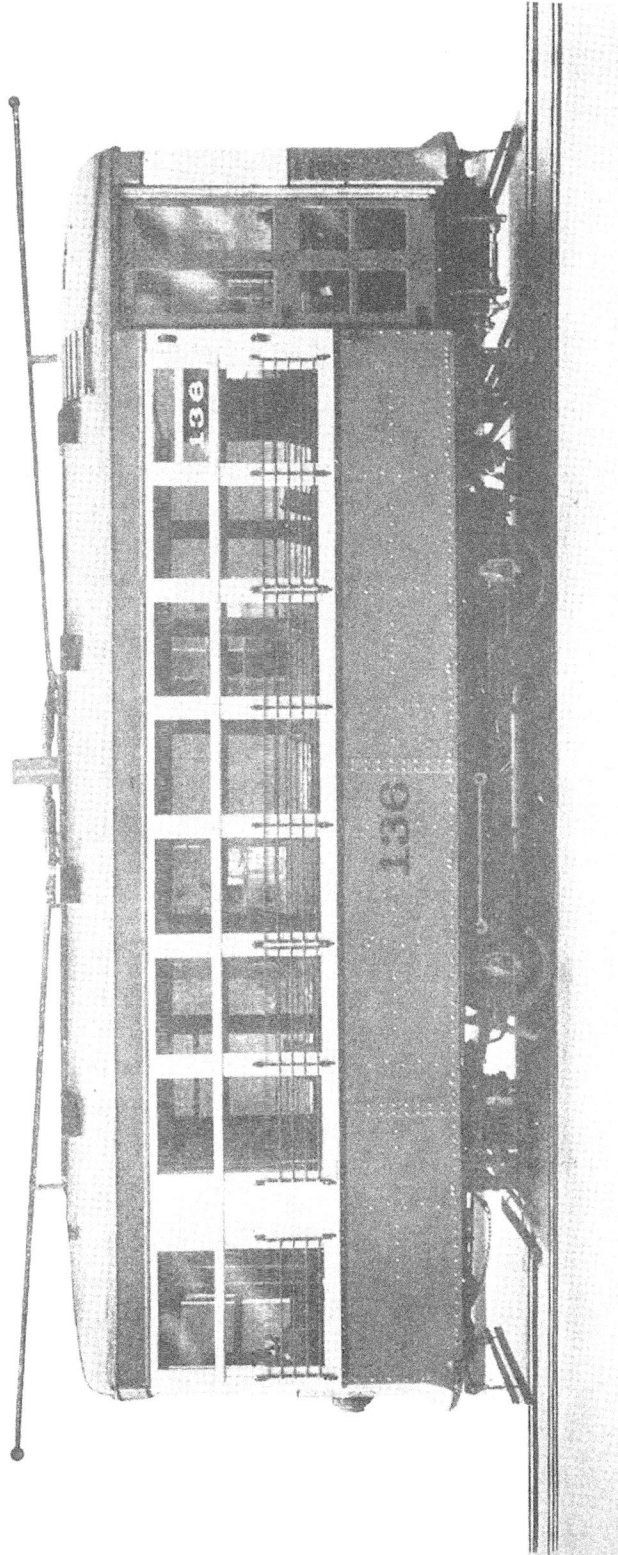

32 PASSENGER—SINGLE TRUCK SAFETY CAR

Halifax Tramways

Dimensions

Length over bumpers	47' 0"
Truck centres	22' 6"
Wheel base	5' 4"
Width of seat	35"
Rail to step	13½"
Step to platform	12"
Seating capacity	52
Width of aisle	27⅝"
Diameter of wheels	26"

Weights and Equipment

Car body and equipment	19,000 lbs.
Trucks and motors	18,000 lbs.
Total	37,000 lbs.
Motors and type, 4 West. No. 510	
H.P. per motor	35.
Control	K

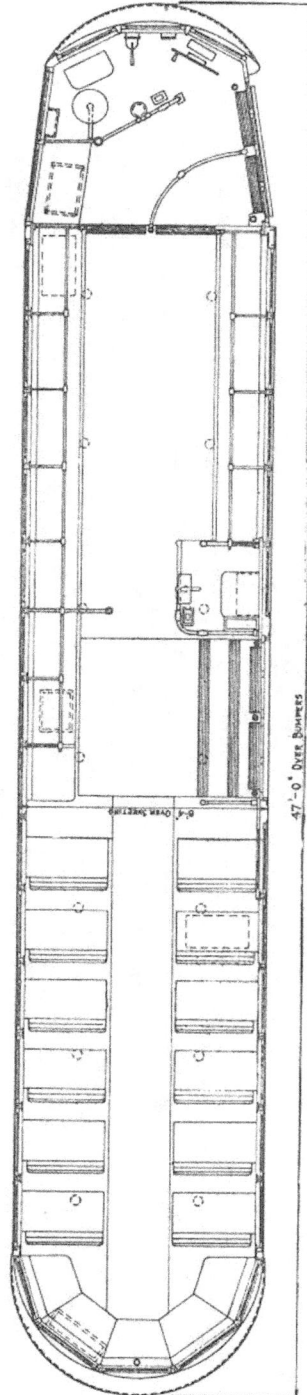

52 PASSENGER PETER WITT CAR

52 PASSENGER PETER WITT CAR

TORONTO TRANSPORTATION COMMISSION

Dimensions

Length over bumpers	42' 7 5/16"
Truck centres	22' 2"
Wheel base	6' 8"
Width of seat	37"
Seating capacity	43
Width of aisle	21¼"
Diameter of wheels	30"
Rail to step	15 3/16" x 3 steps 9" each

Weights and Equipment

Car body and equipment
Trucks and motors..........

Total......... 29,000 lbs.

Motor—4 cyl. 4 cycle v. in h. heavy duty. Bore 4¾" stroke 6".

H.P.—68 H.P. @ 1500 R.P.M.

Gear ratio—4 to 1 First.
1.76 to 1 Second
1 to 1 Third

Control—Foot operated clutch, hand operated gear shift. Hand operated spark and throttle control. Foot accelerator. West. air brakes.

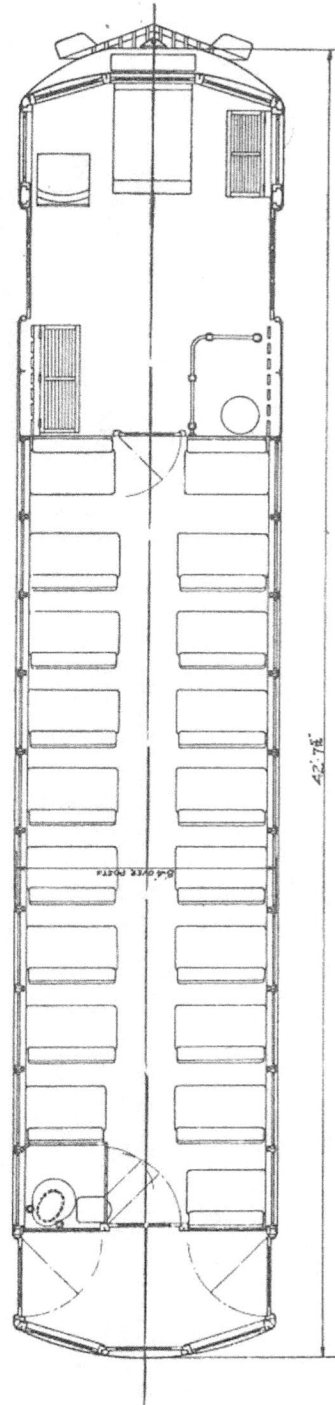

43 PASSENGER GASOLINE CAR
Brill Model No. 55

43 PASSENGER GASOLINE CAR
BRILL MODEL No. 55

Weights and Equipment

Total weight........ 59,000 lbs.

Motor—6 cyl. 4 cycle v. in h.h.d. type. Bore 6" stroke 7".

H.P.—200 H.P.

Control—Foot operated clutch. hand operated gear shift. Hand operated spark and throttle control. West. brakes.

Dimensions

Length over bumpers...... 55' 0"
Truck centres........... 32' 0"
Wheel base............ 8' 4" front
                       7' 0" rear
Width of seat........... 37"
Seating capacity..........56
Width of aisle........... 29¼"
Diameter of wheels........ 33"
Rail to step 15½" x 3 steps of 11¼" each.

56 PASSENGER GASOLINE CAR
BRILL MODEL NO. 75

56 PASSENGER GASOLINE CAR
Brill Model No. 75

WEIGHTS AND EQUIPMENT

Total weight	125,000 lbs
Generator—Westinghouse	500 volt
Gas engine	250 H.P.
Motors—2 West	557-A-8
H. P.	140
Control	Double end

DIMENSIONS:

Length over end sheathing	73' 0"
Truck centres	54' 6"
Wheel base	7' 6" front; 7' 0" rear
Length of seats	51 3/16" and 22 3/16"
Seating Capacity—	
Passenger compartment	56
Smoking compartment	20
Diameter of wheels	33"

BRILL-WESTINGHOUSE GAS ELECTRIC CAR

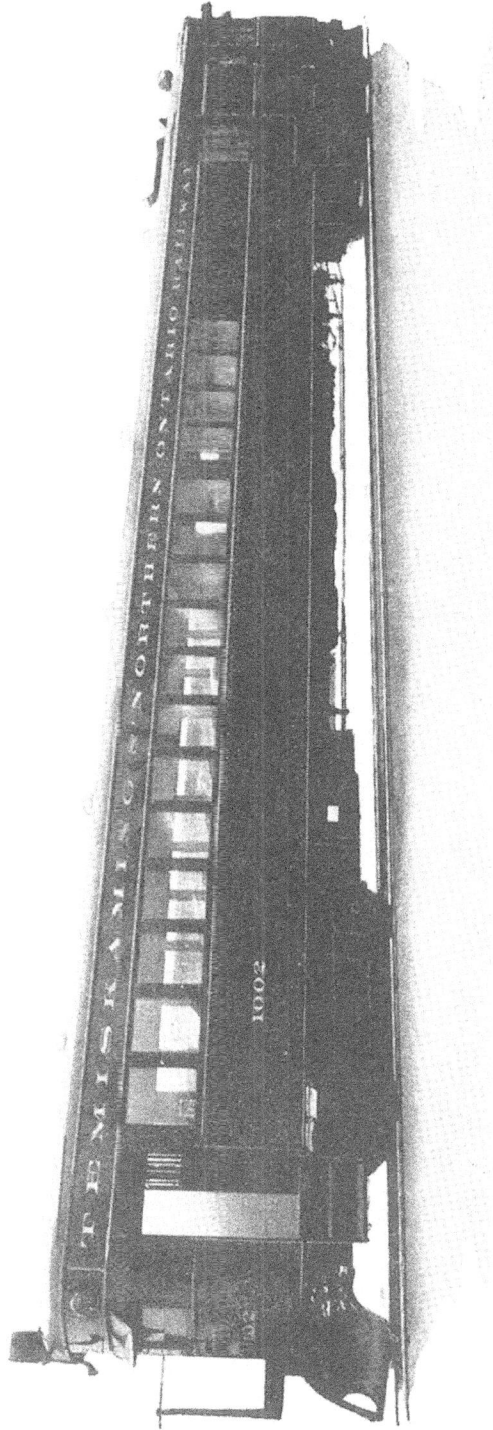

BRILL-WESTINGHOUSE GAS ELECTRIC CAR

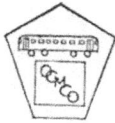

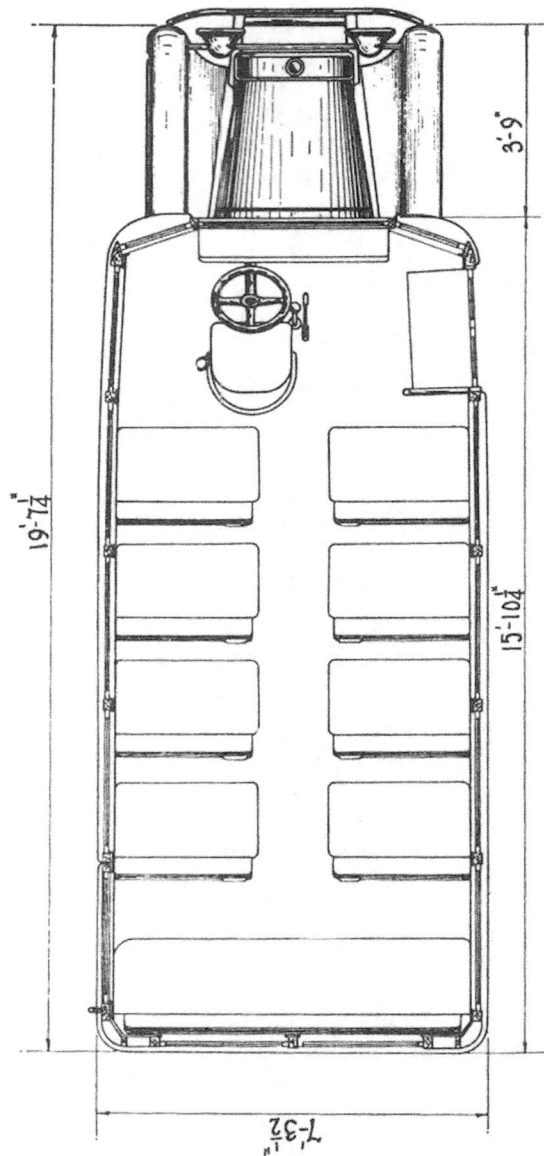

21 Passenger Street Car Bus on Reo "G" Chassis.

Weight: 8300 Lbs.

Seats: Rattan. Deluxe Extra.

Passengers: 21.

Headlining: Agasote.

21 PASSENGER "G" BUS

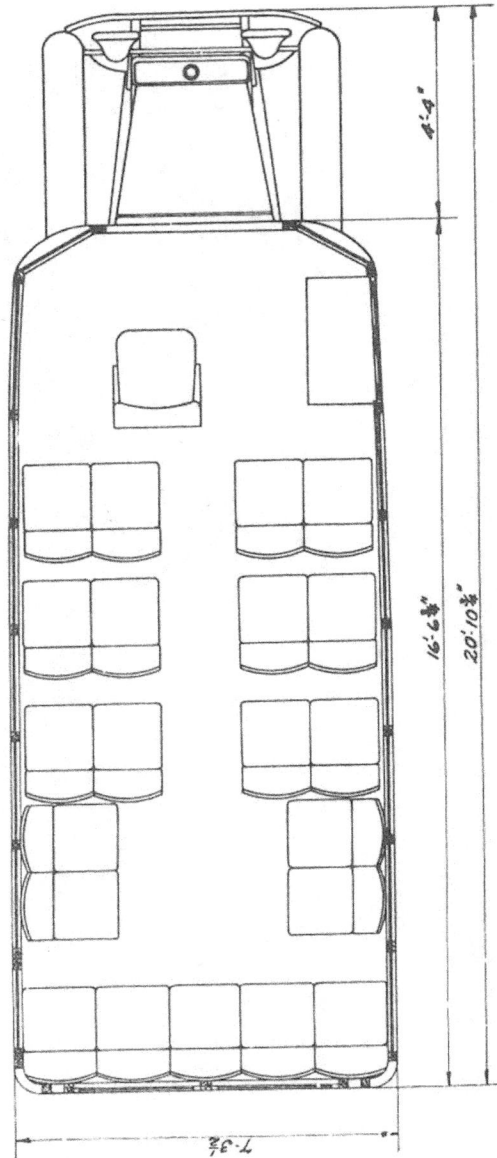

21 PASSENGER STREET CAR BUS ON REO "W" CHASSIS.

Weight: 8300 Lbs.
Seats: Rattan. Deluxe Extra.
Passengers: 21.
Headlining: Agasote.
Curtain Material: Pantasote.

21 PASSENGER "W" BUS

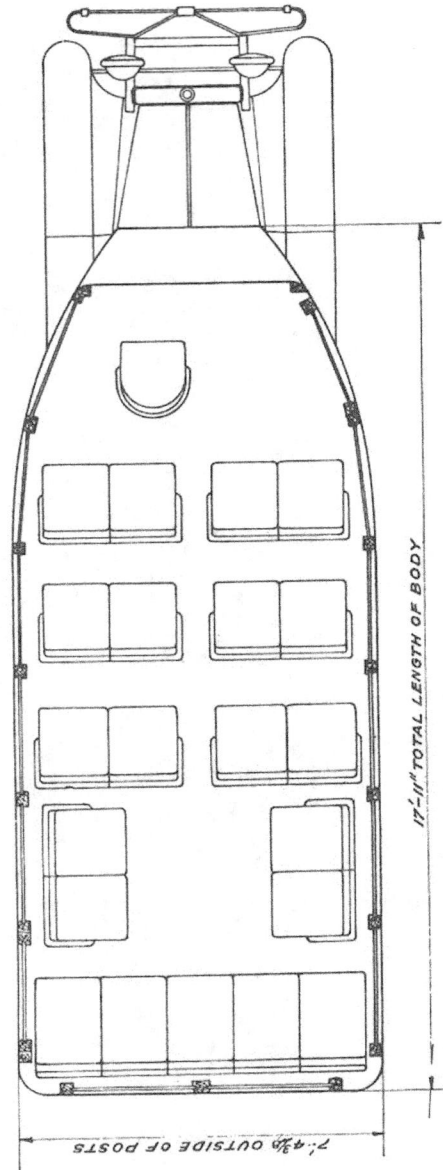

21 PASSENGER CHAIR COACH ON TYPE "W" REO CHASSIS.

WEIGHT: 8300 LBS.

SEATS: WICKER FRAME, LEATHER COVERED.

PASSENGERS: 21.

FLOOR COVERING: CARPET.

CURTAIN MATERIAL: SILK.

HEADLINING: LEATHER.

17'-11" TOTAL LENGTH OF BODY

7'-4⅜ OUTSIDE OF POSTS

21 PASSENGER CHAIR COACH "W"

31"

$\frac{5}{16}$

$\frac{5}{16}$

$18\frac{3}{4}$"

2'-11"

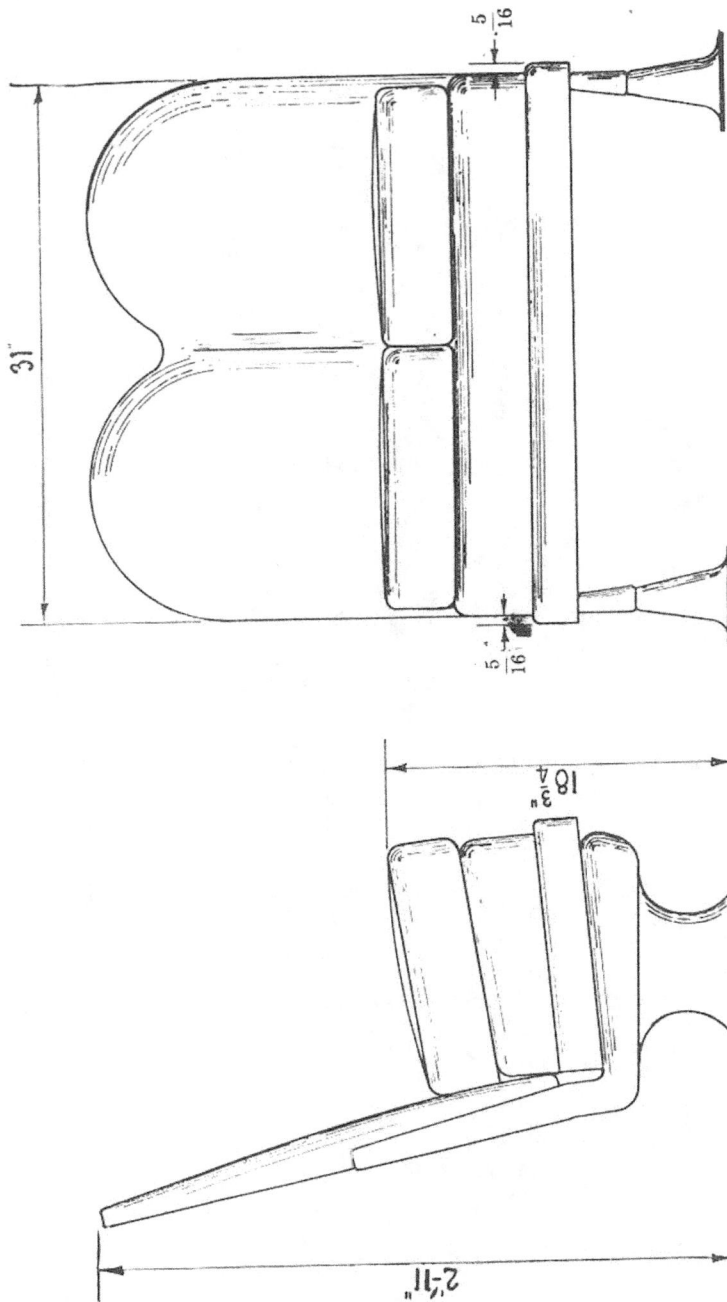

BUS CROSS SEAT—DE LUXE AIR TYPE.

No. 300.   BUS TYPE

Dimensions...........Standard dimensions on reverse side of page.
Overall length........As specified.
Upholstery...........Genuine leather, or as specified.
Back................Slightly recessed.
Cushion.............Upper cushion, springs and stuffed, known as air type.
                     Lower, deep springs, having felt on top,
                     covered all over.
Pedestal.............Pressed steel.
Aisle and wall plates...Pressed steel.
Seat braces..........Steel angle.

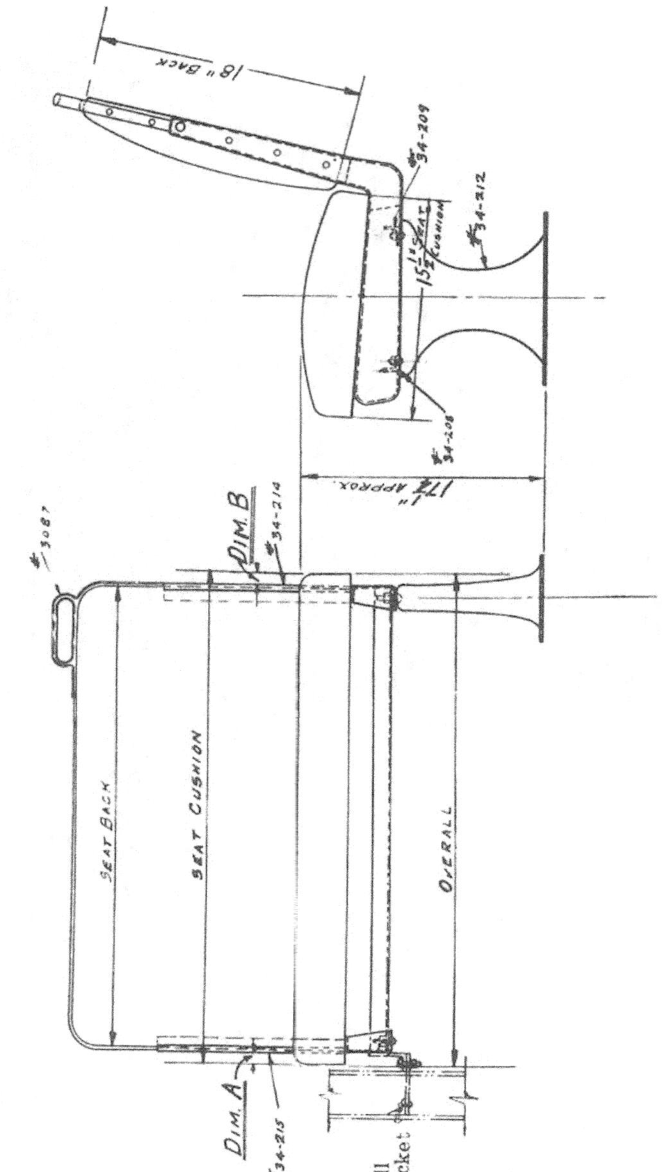

STANDARD STATIONARY CROSS SEAT
Spring Upholstered
No. 100-A

STANDARD STATIONARY CROSS SEAT

Dimensions. . . . . . .Standard dimensions on reverse side of page.
Overall length. . . . .As specified.
Upholstery. . . . . . .Twill woven rattan, or as specified.
Back. . . . . .Slightly recessed, and stuffed.
Grab handle. . . . . . Top corner type.
Cushion. . . . . .Standard Streetcar type.
Pedestal. . . . . .Pressed steel.
Aisle and wall plates—Pressed steel.
Seat braces. . . . . . .Steel angle.

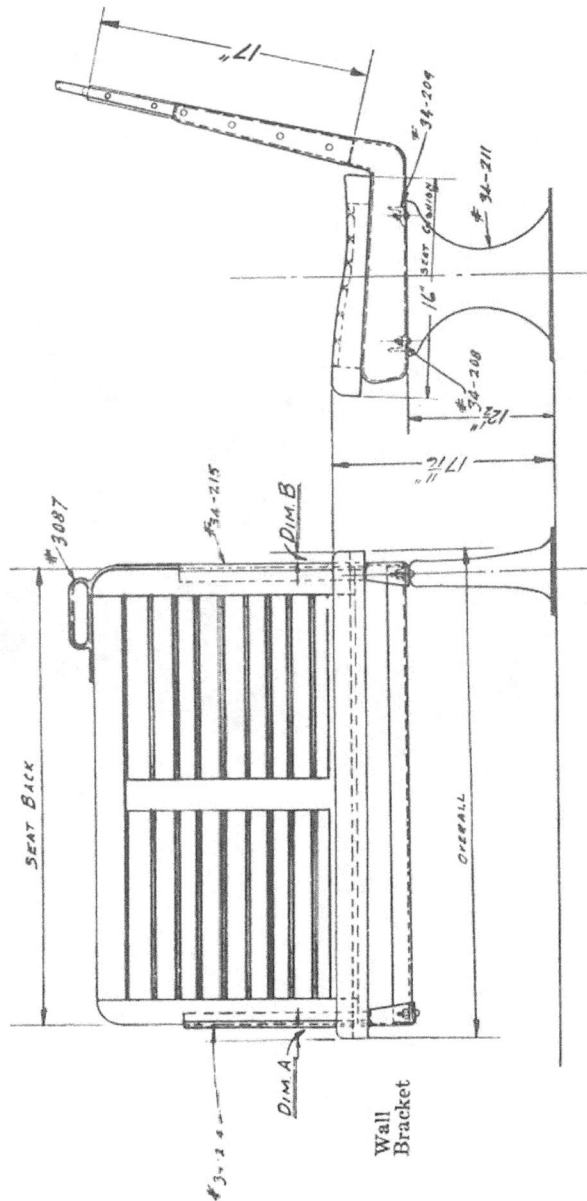

STANDARD STATIONARY SLAT SEAT
No. 100-B

STANDARD STATIONARY SLAT SEAT

Dimensions...... Standard dimensions on reverse side of page.
Overall length.....As specified.
Cushion and back Made in birch, stained to suit interior car.
Pedestal..........Pressed steel.
Aisle and wall plates—Pressed steel.
Seat braces....... Single angle, to allow cushion to lift up.
Grab handle...... Corner grab, or as shown.

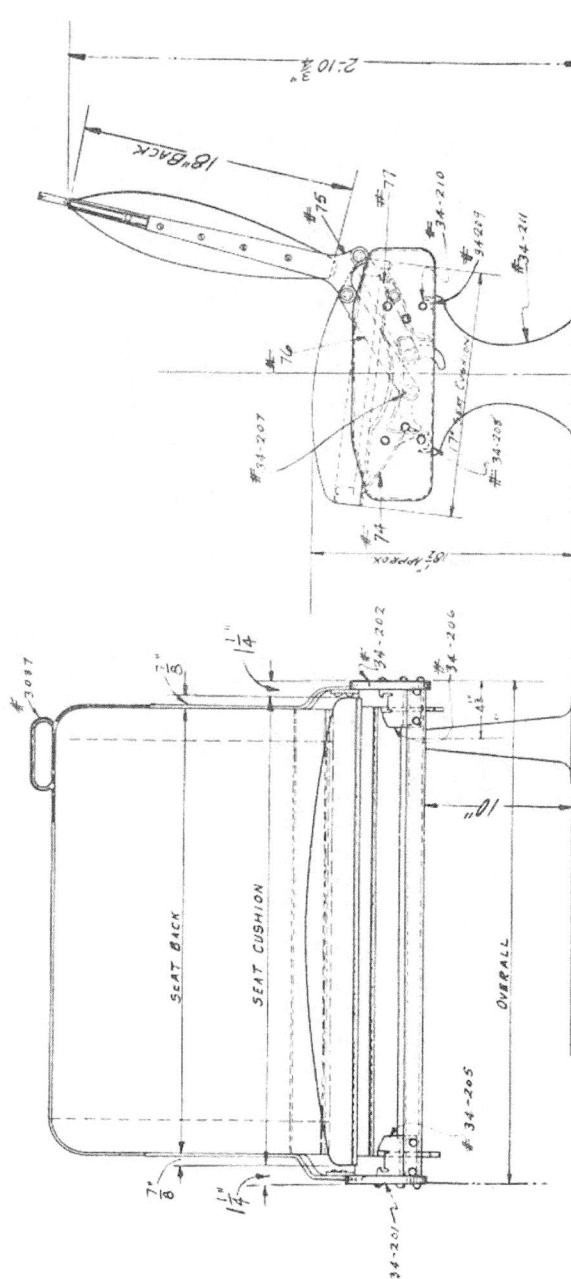

STANDARD REVERSIBLE SEAT—SPRING UPHOLSTERED
No. 200-A

SEAT BACK

SEAT CUSHION

OVERALL

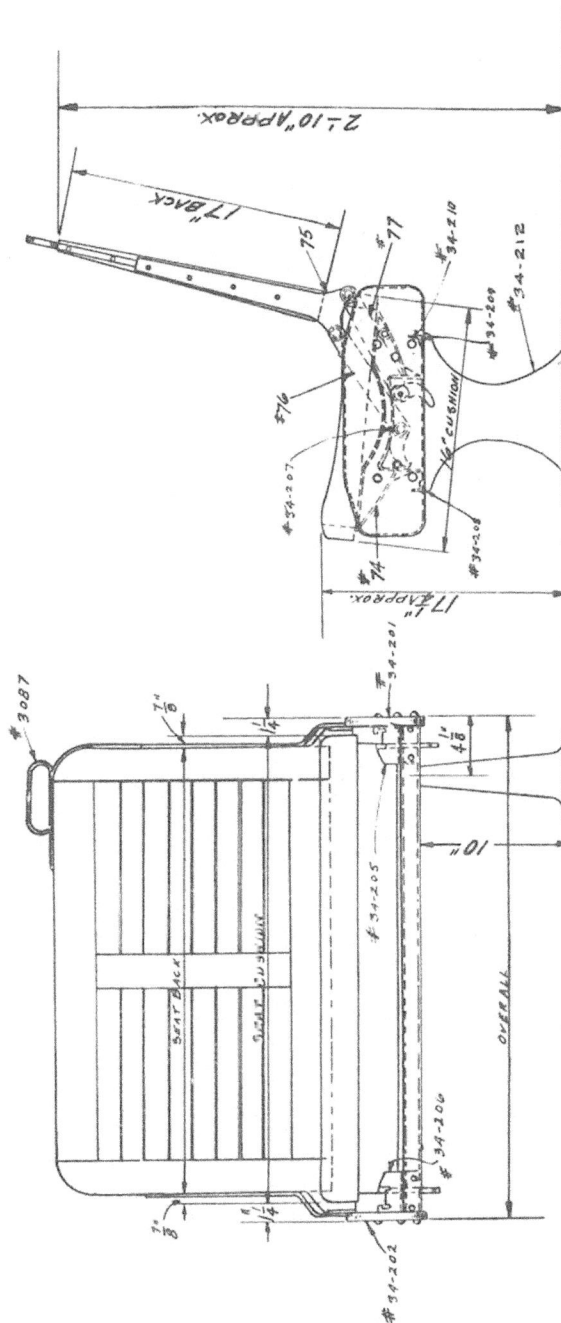

STANDARD REVERSIBLE SLAT SEAT
No. 200-B

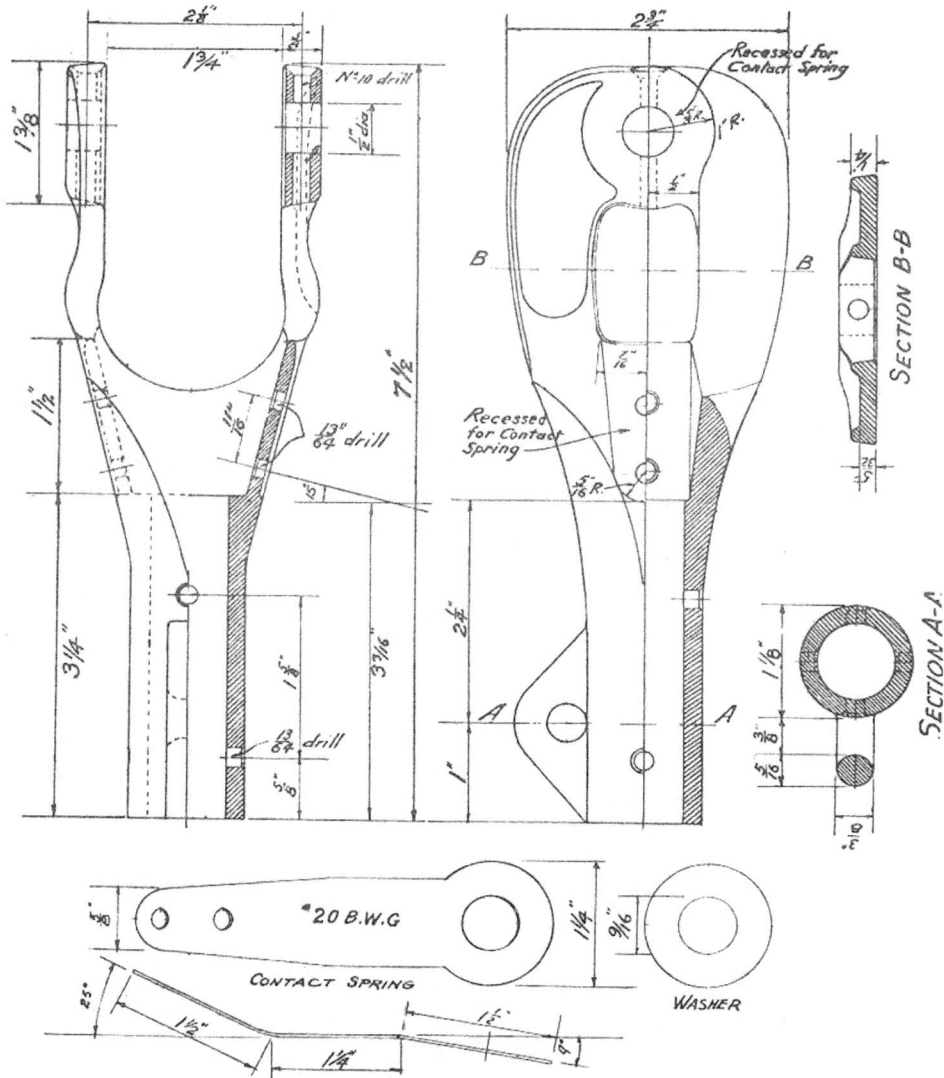

TROLLEY HARP.
No. 612
MALLEABLE IRON.

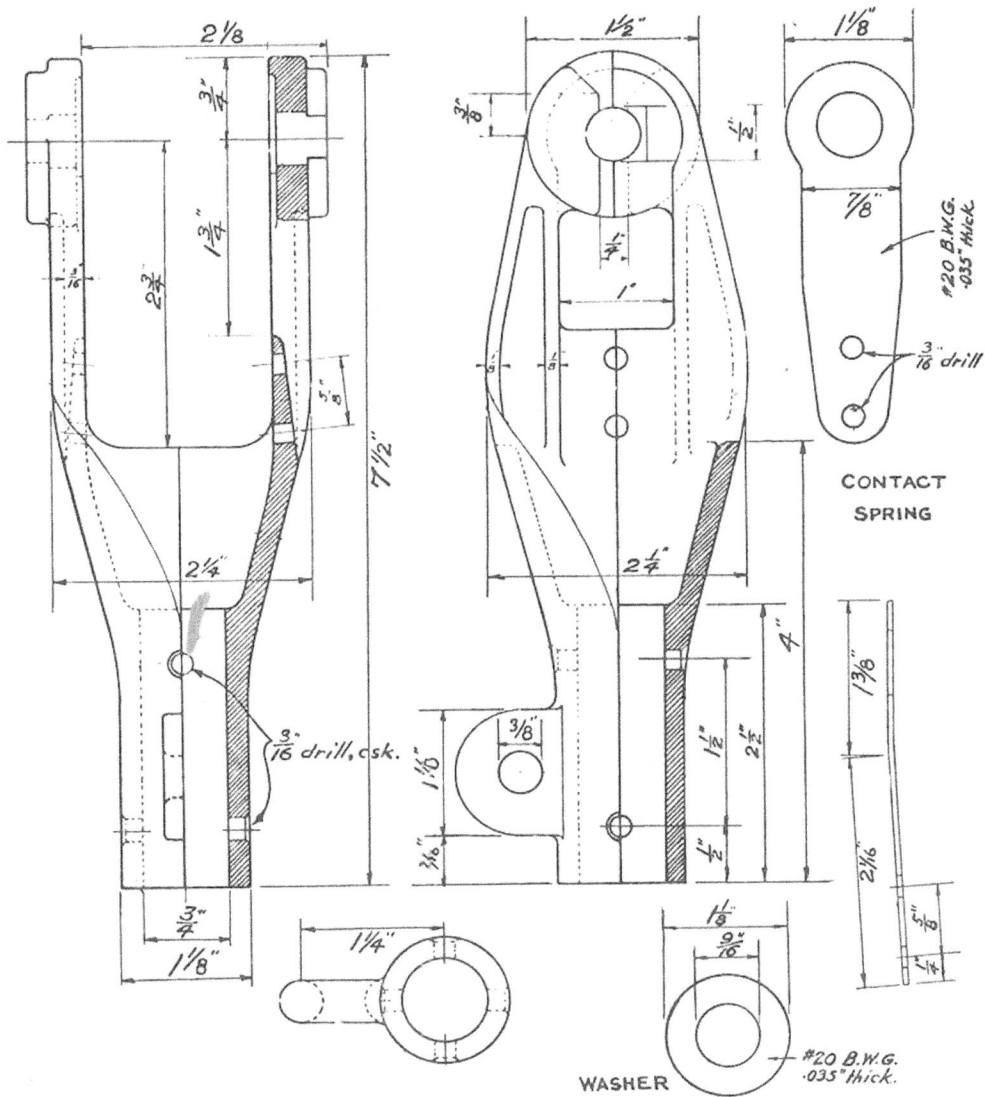

CONTACT
SPRING

WASHER

MATERIAL

TROLLEY HARP.
No. 614
MALLEABLE IRON.

Hole in Handle filled with Wax

#14-20 Special Mach Bolt 5" long

$4\frac{5}{16}$"

$7\frac{1}{16}$"

$5\frac{1}{16}$" (Turned Wood handle)

Take Size of hole off Rod.

Note:- Boss to be cut off to dotted line for for selective control.

HANDLE FOR CONDUCTORS' DOOR CONTROL
No. 3192
BRONZE CRANK—WOOD HANDLE.

$3\frac{5}{8}$"

$4\frac{11}{16}$"

$8\frac{5}{16}$"

CONDUCTORS' DOOR CONTROL HANDLE FOR SELECTIVE
DOOR CONTROL
No. 3249
BRONZE CRANK—WOOD HANDLE

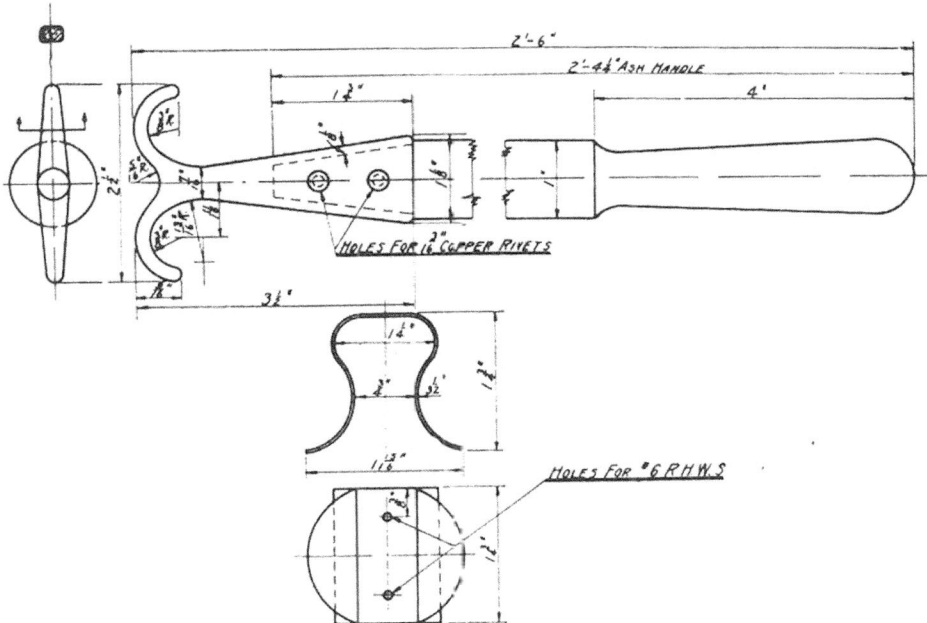

VENTILATOR OPENER
No. 3196

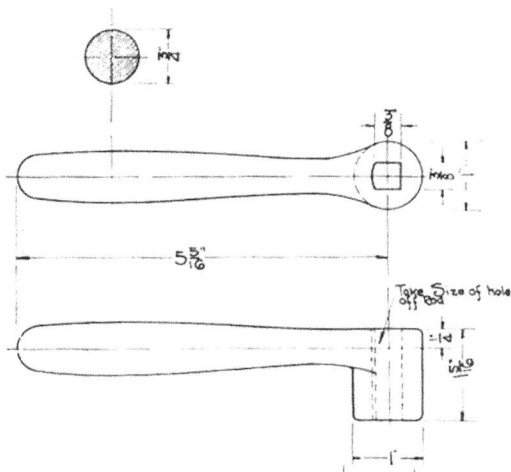

HANDLE FOR CONDUCTORS' DOOR CONTROL
No. 3193
BRONZE

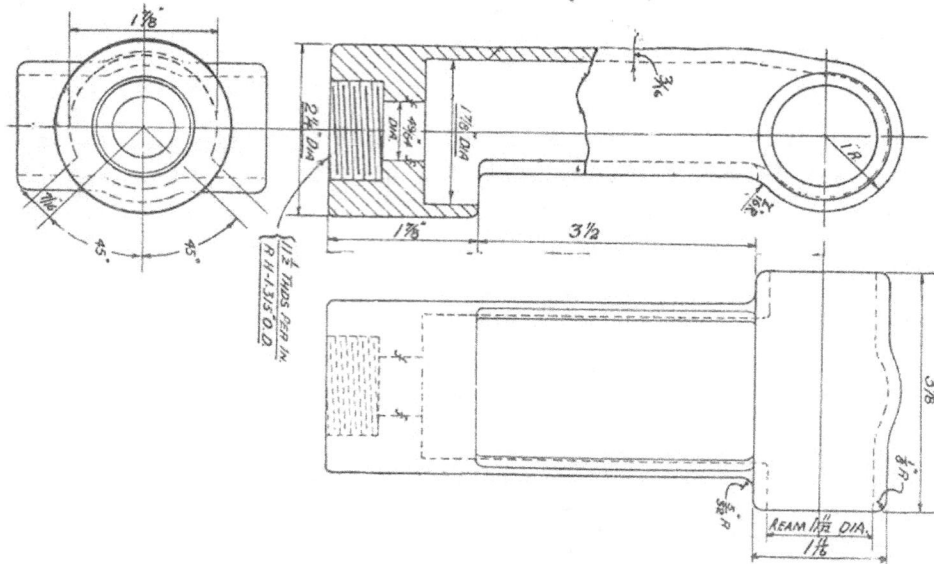

HANDLE HOUSING FOR CONDUCTOR'S
DOOR CONTROL
No. 3216
ALUMINUM

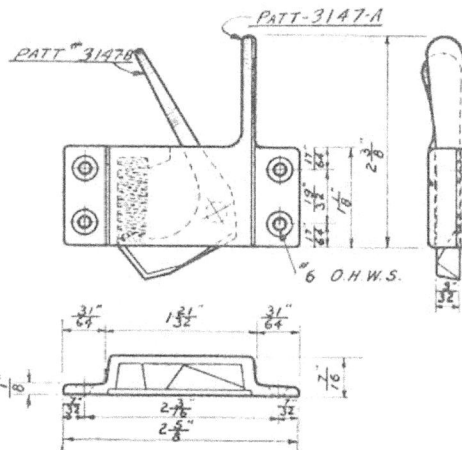

SASH LOCK—RIGHT HAND
No. 3147-A
No. 3147C.   LEFT HAND.
BRONZE

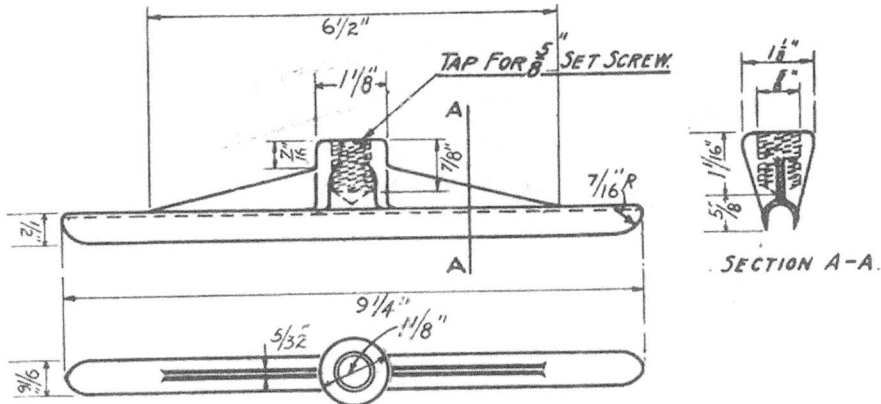

9" TROLLEY EAR
SPECIAL BRONZE
2-O. WIRE

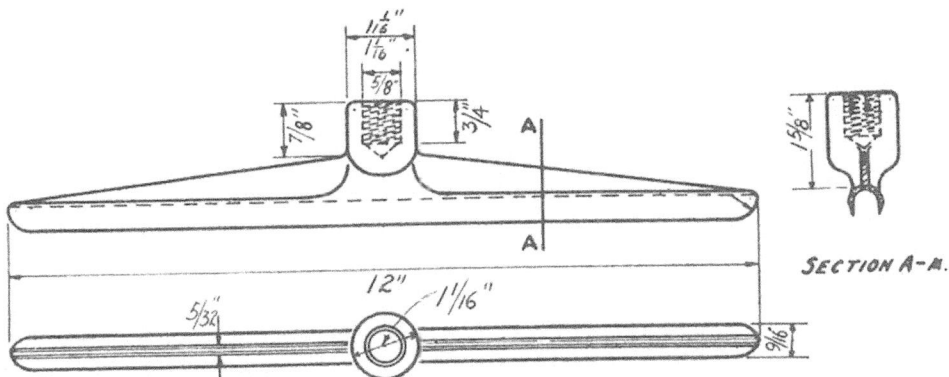

12 INCH TROLLEY EARS
SPECIAL BRONZE
2-O. WIRE

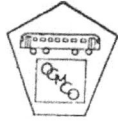

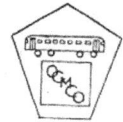

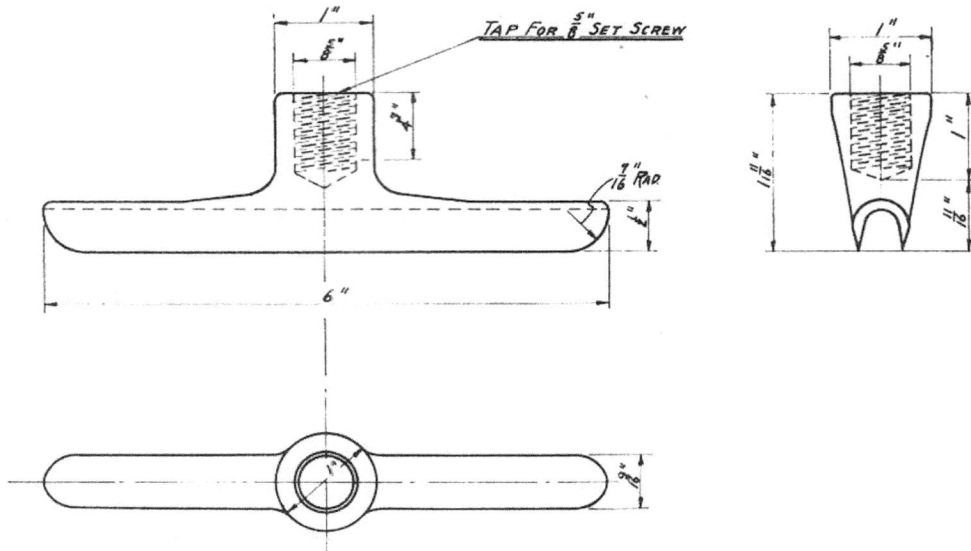

6" TROLLEY EAR
SPECIAL BRONZE
2-O WIRE

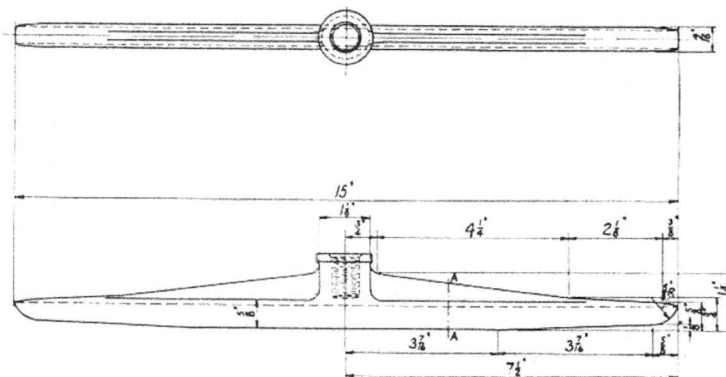

15" TROLLEY EAR
SPECIAL BRONZE
2-O WIRE

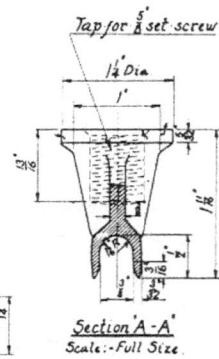

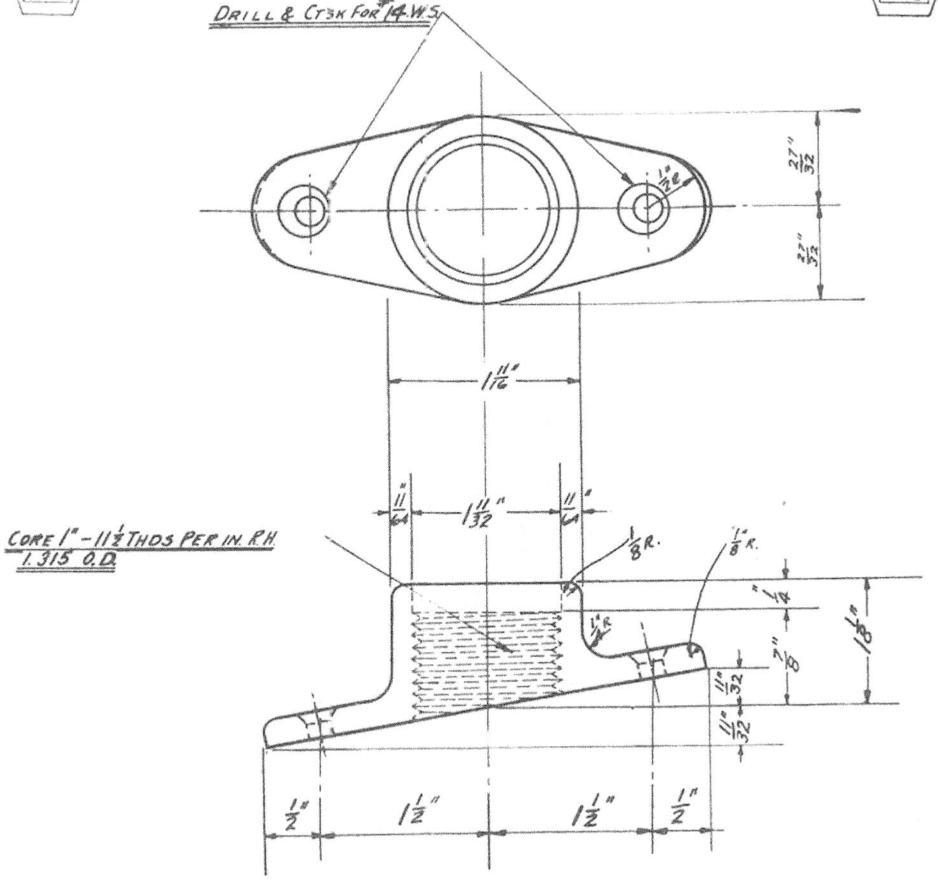
DRILL & CT'SK FOR #14 W.S.
27"/32
27"/32
1 11/16"
11/64"
1 11/32"
11/64"
CORE 1" - 11½ THDS PER IN. R.H. 1.315 O.D.
1/8 R.
1/8" R.
1/4"
1 1/8"
7/8"
11/32"
11/32"
1/2"
1 1/2"
1 1/2"
1/2"

CEILING STANCHION SOCKET BEVEL No. 3141

BRONZE, ALUMINUM OR MALLEABLE IRON

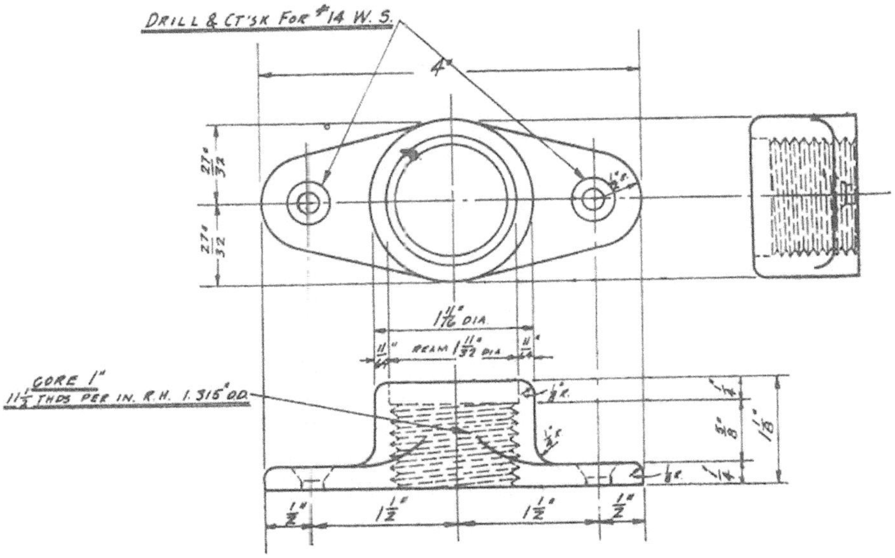
DRILL & CT'SK FOR #14 W.S.
4"
27"/32
27"/32
1 11/16" DIA.
REAM 1 11/32" DIA.
CORE 1"
11½ THDS PER IN. R.H. 1.315" O.D.
1/8 R.
1/4"
5/8"
1 1/8"
1/4"
1/2"
1 1/2"
1 1/2"
1/2"

CEILING STANCHION SOCKET, SQUARE No. 3143

BRONZE, ALUMINUM OR MALLEABLE IRON

REAM TO NEAT FIT (FROM END TO END OF FITTING) FOR 1 5/16" DIA. TUBE.

CORED 1"
11 1/2 THDS PER IN. R.H. 1.315" O.D.

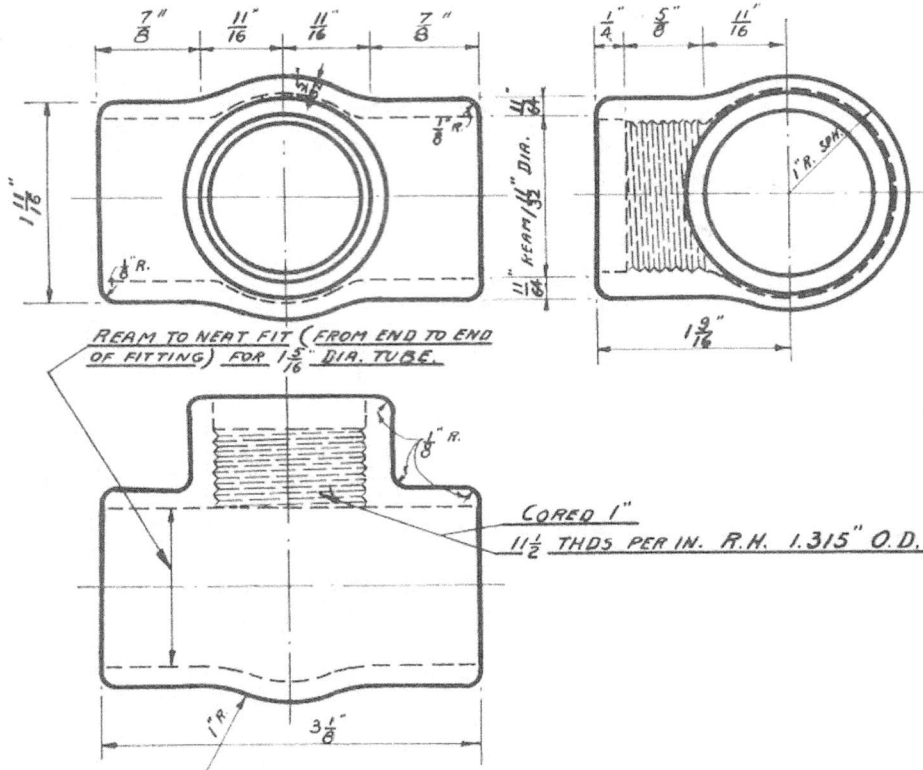

STANCHION TEE.
No. 3144
Bronze, Aluminum or Malleable Iron.

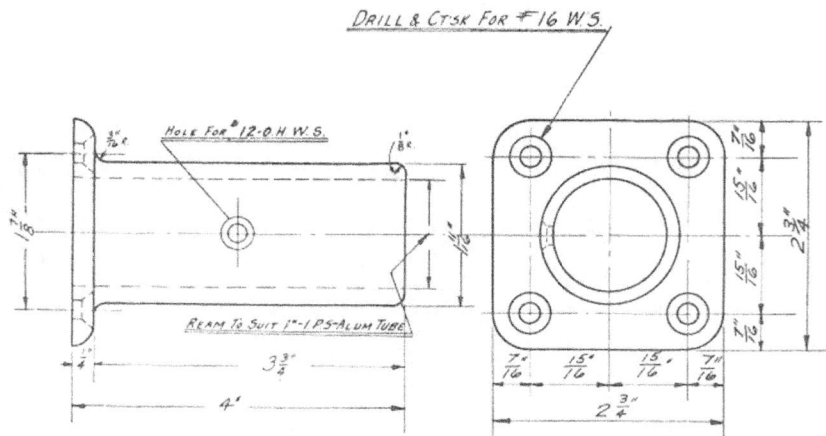

DRILL & CT·SK FOR #16 W.S.

HOLE FOR #12·O.H W.S.

REAM TO SUIT 1"·I P S·ALUM TUBE

STANCHION FLOOR SOCKET
No. 2123
Bronze, Aluminum or Malleable Iron

11½ THDS. PER IN. R.H. 1.315" O.D.

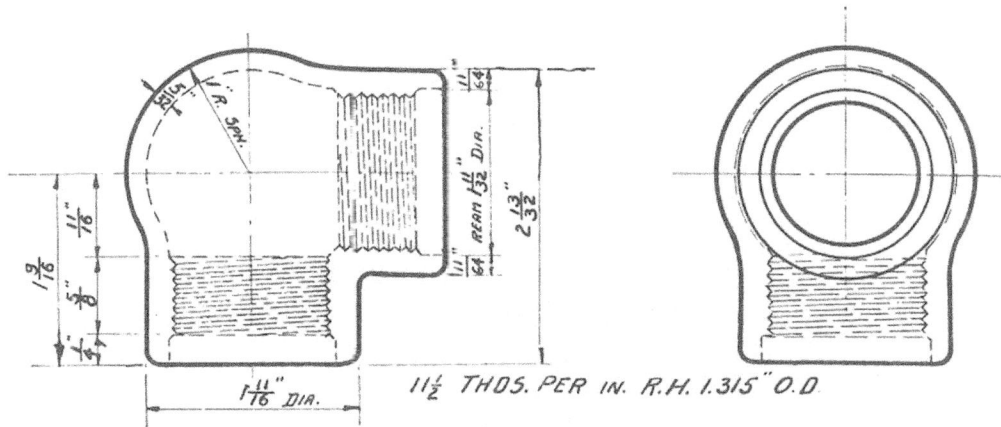

STANCHION ELBOW
No. 3145
BRONZE, ALUMINUM OR MALLEABLE IRON

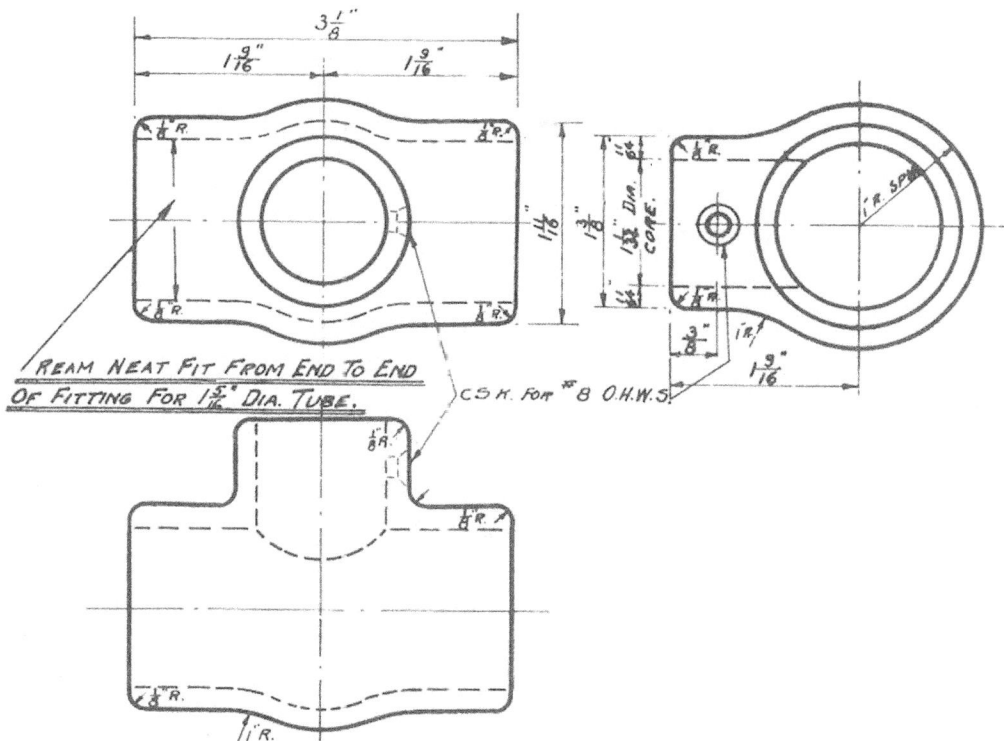

REAM NEAT FIT FROM END TO END
OF FITTING FOR 1⅝" DIA. TUBE.

CSK. FOR #8 O.H.W.S.

STANCHION REDUCING TEE FOR HANDPOLE.
No. 3148
BRONZE, ALUMINUM OR MALLEABLE IRON.

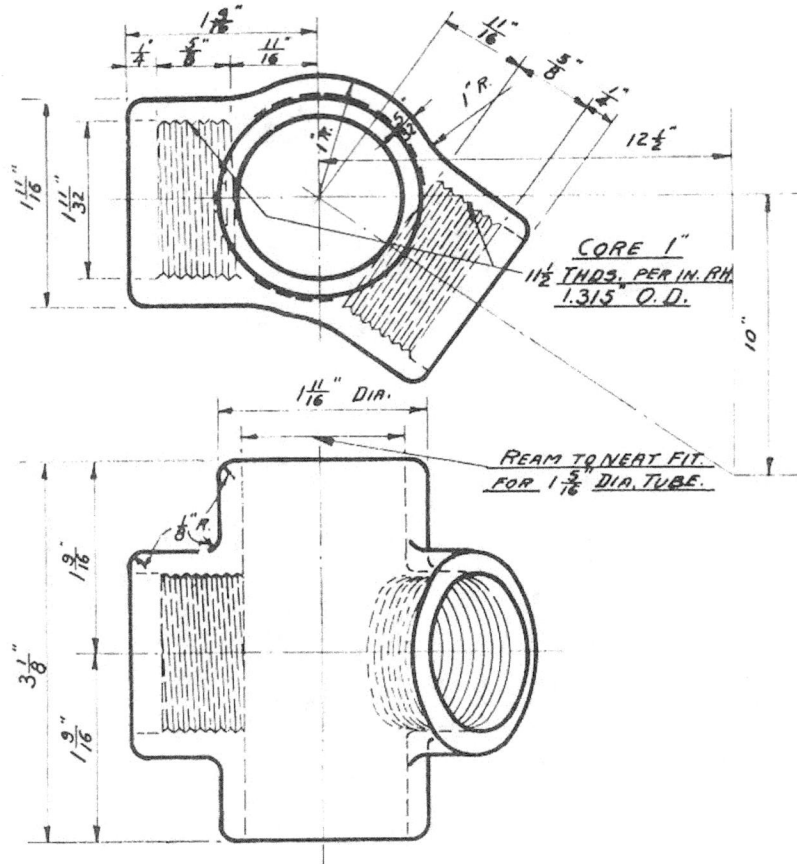

CORE 1"
11½ THDS. PER IN. R.H.
1.315" O.D.

REAM TO NEAT FIT.
FOR 1 5/16" DIA. TUBE.

STANCHION ANGLE CROSS
No. 3146
BRONZE, ALUMINUM OR MALLEABLE IRON.

DRILL & CSK FOR #14 W.S.

4 3/8"

2 3/16"

1/8" R.

7/8"

2 1/4"

1 3/8"

1/4"

1/2"

11/64" REAM 1 11/32" DIA. 11/64"

1 11/16" DIA.

CORE 1" 11 1/2 THDS. PER IN. R.H. 1.315" O.D.

4"

27/32"

1 11/16"

27/32"

BULKHEAD STANCHION SOCKET, BEVEL
No. 3154
ALUMINUM, BRONZE OR MALLEABLE IRON

1 3/8"

1 11/16"

1 13/16"

1 15/16" R.

5/8"

1/2"

1 3/8" DIA.

1 11/16" DIA.

HOLES DRILLED & C.S.K. FOR #14 W.S.

1/8" R.

27/32"

27/32"

2 1/2"

1 1/4"

CORE 1"
11 1/2 THDS. PER IN R.H. 1.315" O.D.

4"

3/16"

1/4" 1 1/4" 1 1/2" 1/4"

No. 277   STANCHION SOCKET
(ABOVE DOOR)
ALUMINUM, BRONZE OR MALLEABLE IRON

STANCHION CROSS
No. 3270
BRONZE, ALUMINUM OR MALLEABLE IRON

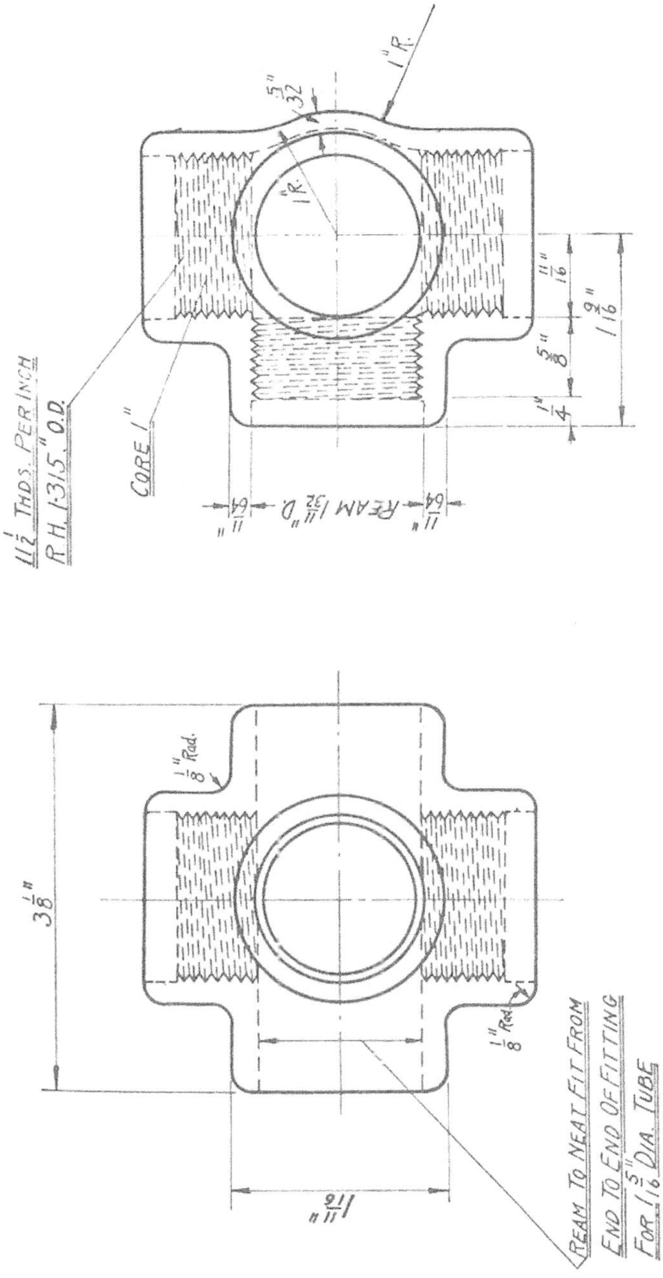

SIDE OUTLET CROSS
No. 3178
BRONZE, ALUMINUM OR MALLEABLE IRON

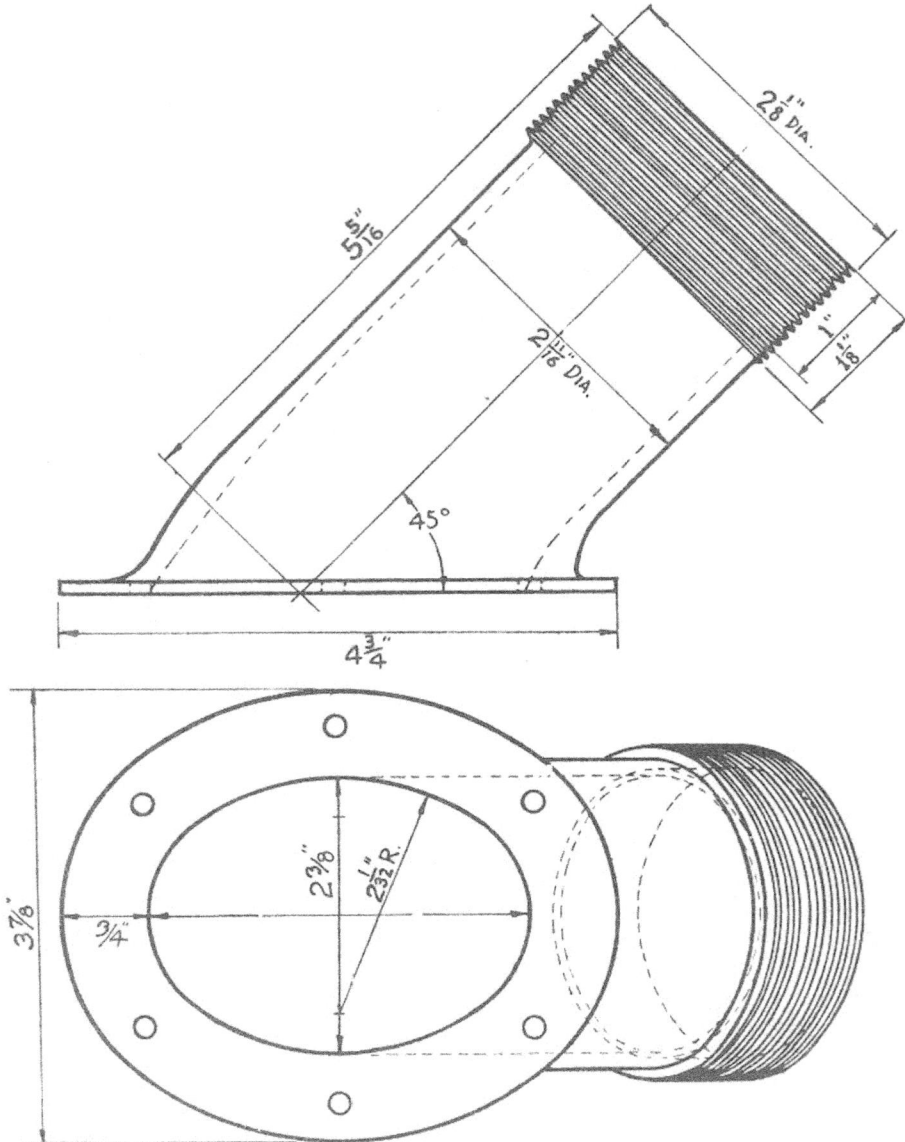

FILLER FLANGE FOR GAS TANK
ALUMINUM
STREET CAR BUS
3269

ALL OUTER SURFACES TO BE BUFFED

4 5/32 DRILLED HOLES

7/32"

3 5/8" φ

5/8"

1/8"

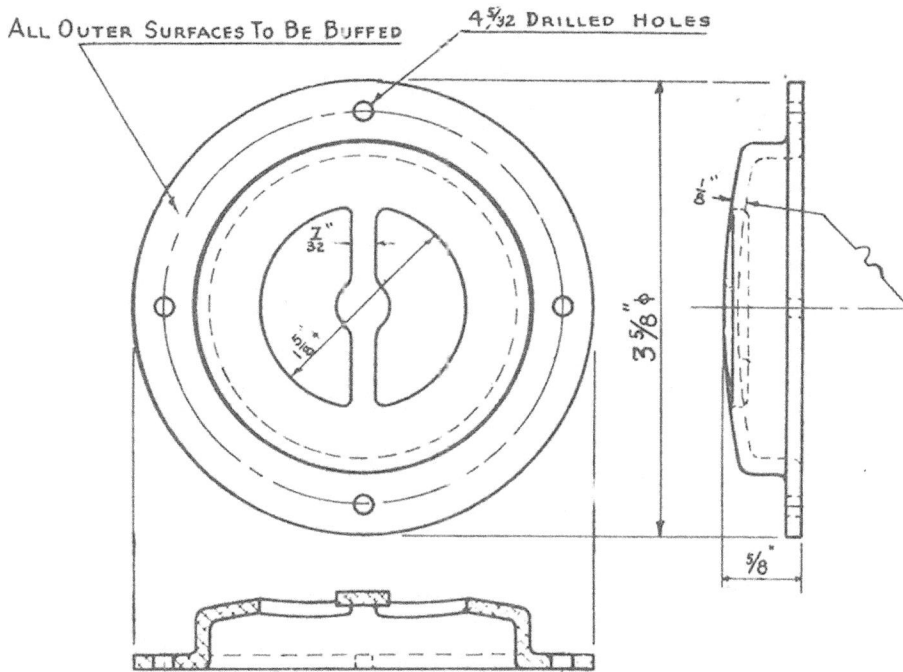

GUARD OVER GASOLINE GAUGE
ALUMINUM
STREET CAR BUS
No. 3277

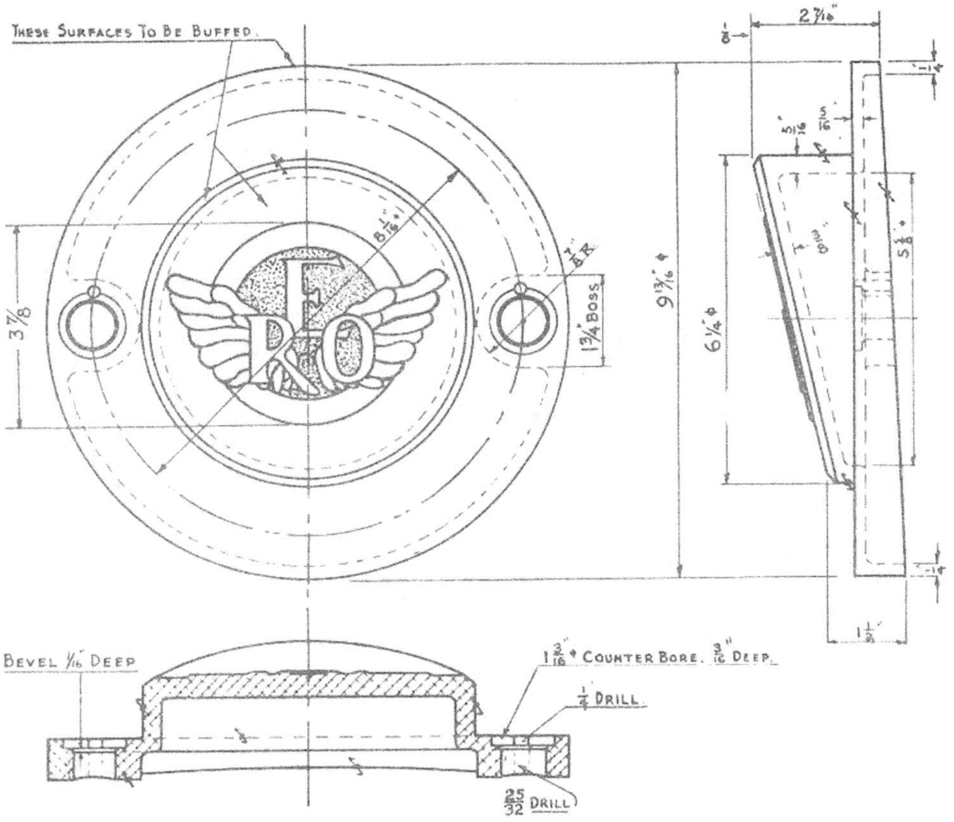
These Surfaces To Be Buffed
2 7/16"
9 13/16"
6 1/4"
3 7/8
1 3/4 Boss
Bevel 1/16" Deep
1 3/16" Counter Bore, 3/16" Deep
1/4" Drill
25/32 Drill

SPARE TIRE CARRIER

ALUMINUM

21 PASS. STREET CAR BUS

ON TYPE "G" AND "W" CHASSIS

NO. 3276

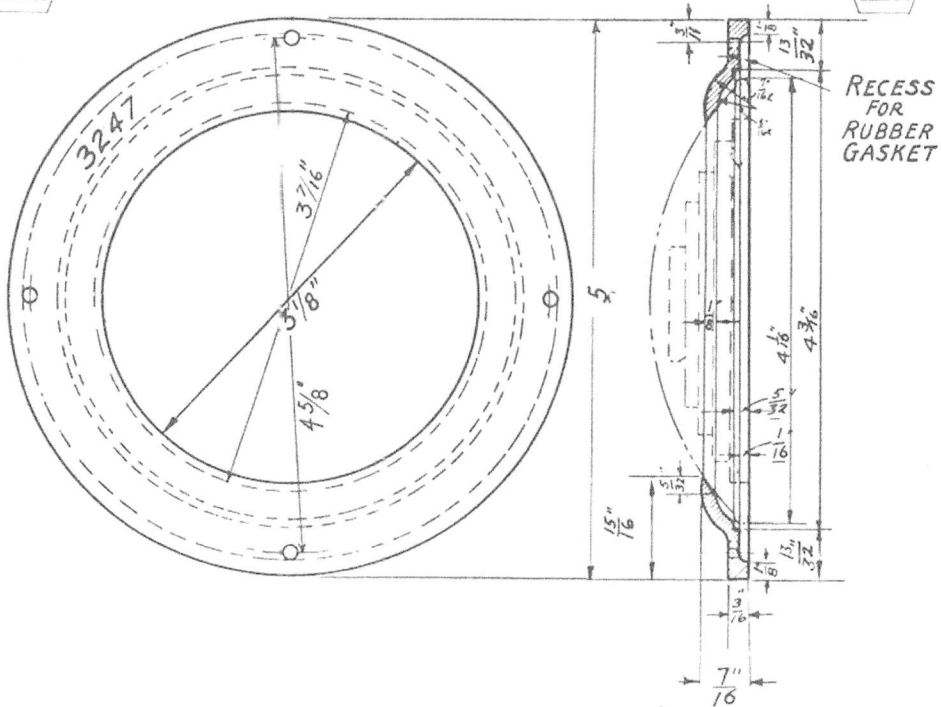

RETAINER FOR MARKER LIGHT LENS
Aluminum
For use with Rubber Gasket
No. 3247

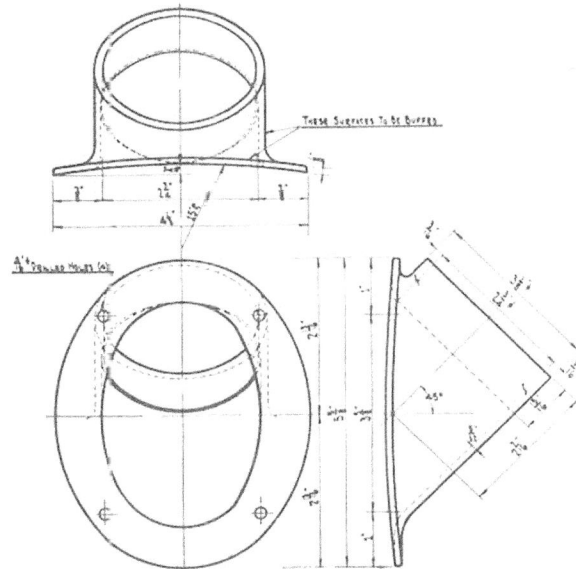

RECESS FOR RUBBER GASKET

FLANGE FOR GASOLINE FILLER TUBE
Aluminum
TO BODY OF BUS
No. 3271

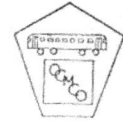

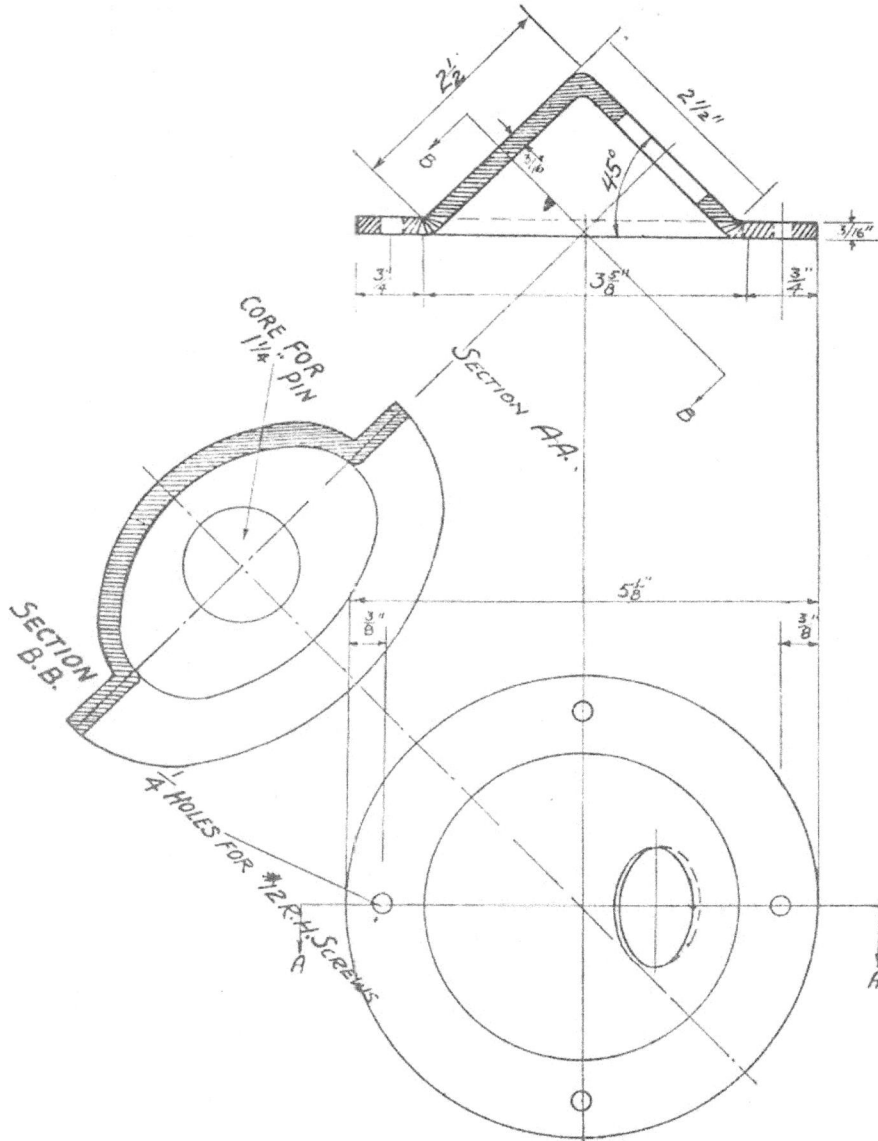

DROP PIN HOUSING
MALLEABLE IRON
No. 3157

8 1/4"

A

A

$\frac{9}{32}$"

9/32"

$1\frac{1}{32}$" R.

3/16 R

3"/16 R

HOLES TO BE DRILLED & C.T.S.K.
FOR "10 O.H.W.S.

2" R.

2"

$\frac{7}{32}$"

HOLES TO BE DRILLED
& C.T.S.K. FOR "10 O.H.W.S.

7/8" R.

9 1/2" Max.

B   B

$\frac{3}{4}$"

$\frac{7}{32}$"

SECTION B-B.

$\frac{3}{4}$"

$2\frac{3}{32}$"

$\frac{7}{8}$ R.

$\frac{3}{4}$"

$\frac{3}{4}$ R

SECTION A-A.

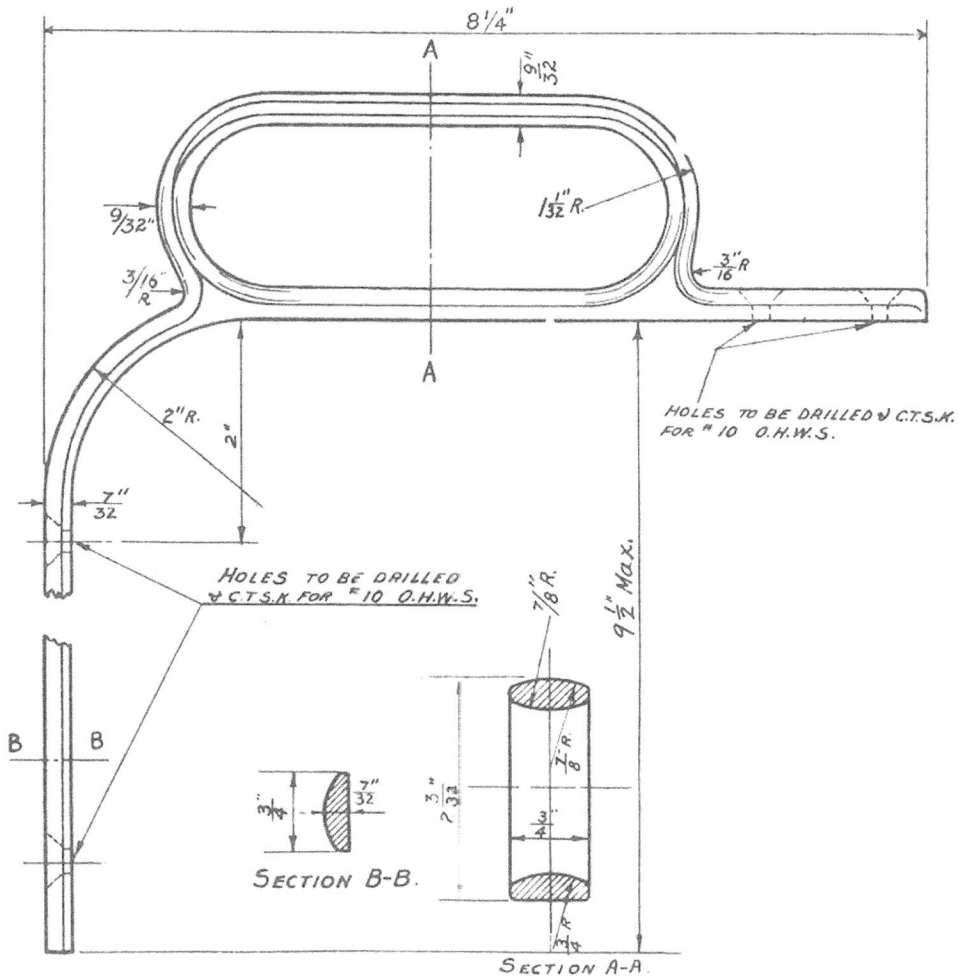

STANDARD SEAT BACK CORNER GRAB HANDLE
Bronze or Aluminum
No. 3087

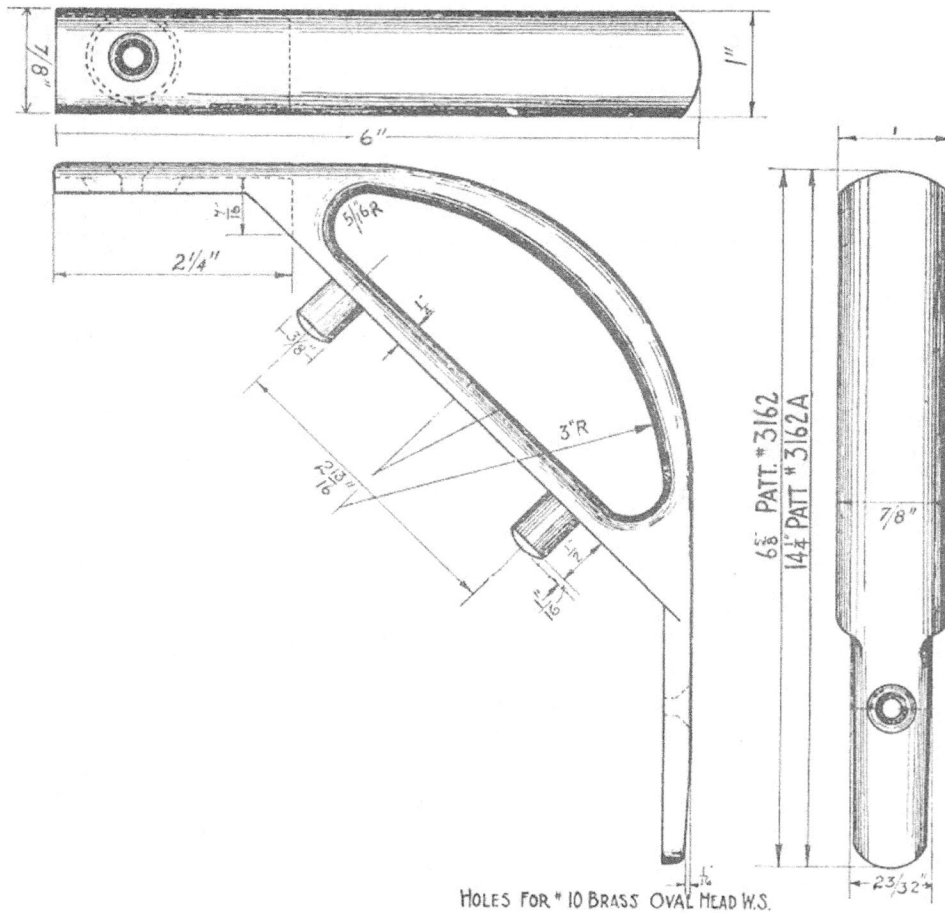

HOLES FOR # 10 BRASS OVAL HEAD W.S.

SEAT GRAB HANDLE
BRONZE OR ALUMINUM
No. 3162 and 3162A

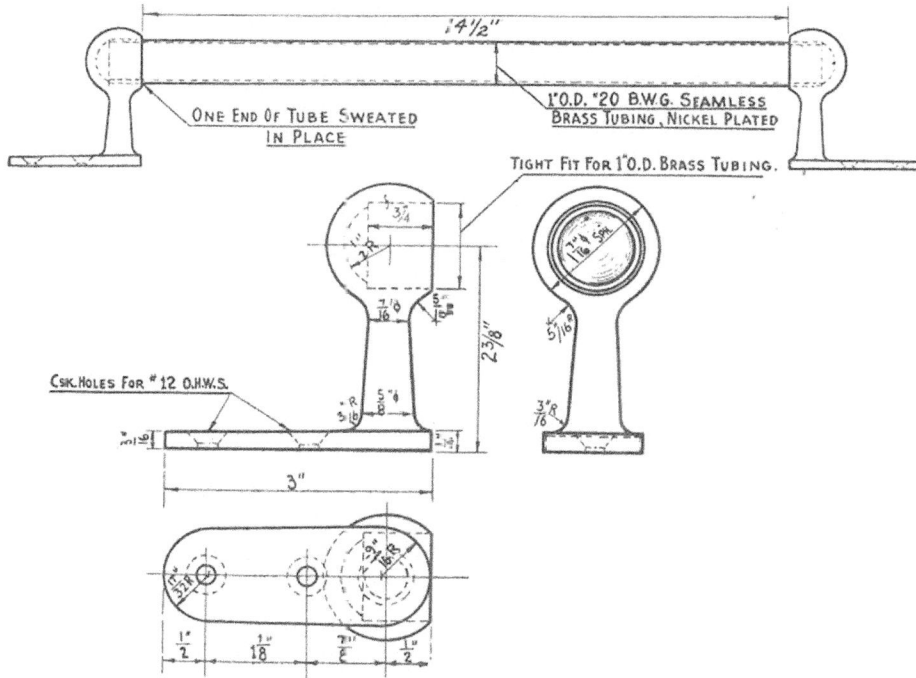

14 1/2"

ONE END OF TUBE SWEATED
IN PLACE

1" O.D. #20 B.W.G. SEAMLESS
BRASS TUBING, NICKEL PLATED

TIGHT FIT FOR 1" O.D. BRASS TUBING.

3/4

CSK. HOLES FOR #12 O.H.W.S.

3"

GRAB HANDLE WITH STRAIGHT POSTS
STREET CAR BUS
No. 3272
BRASS CASTING—NICKLE PLATED

15"

ONE END OF TUBE SWEATED IN PLACE.

1" O.D. #20 B.W.G. SEAMLESS BRASS
TUBING, NICKEL PLATED.

TIGHT FIT FOR 1" O.D. BRASS TUBING

$\frac{9}{16}$"

$2\frac{5}{16}$"

$2\frac{9}{16}$"

$\frac{5}{16}$R

$\frac{5}{16}$R

$2\frac{1}{2}$R

$2\frac{5}{32}$

$1\frac{1}{16}$"

$1\frac{1}{2}$

$\frac{11}{32}$R

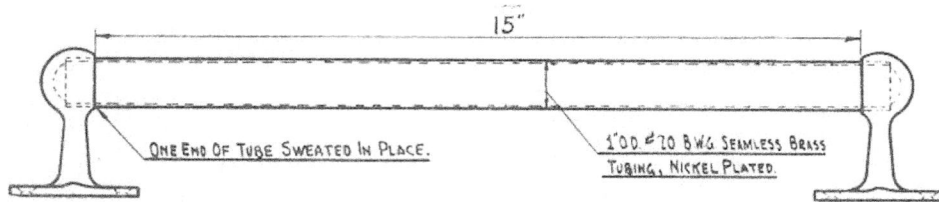

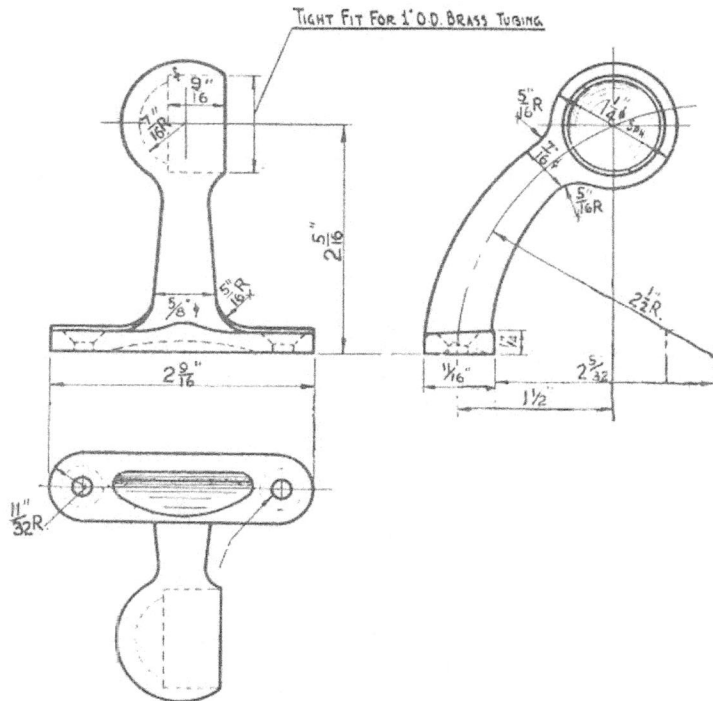

GRAB HANDLE WITH OFFSET POSTS
STREET CAR BUS
No. 3273-R.   3273-L.
BRASS CASTING, NICKLE PLATED.

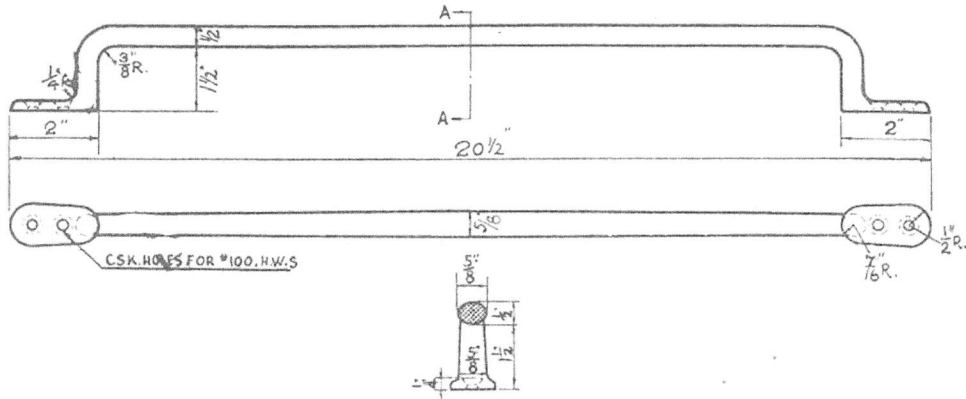

GRAB HANDLE ON PARTITION
STREET CAR BUS
No. 3274
BRASS

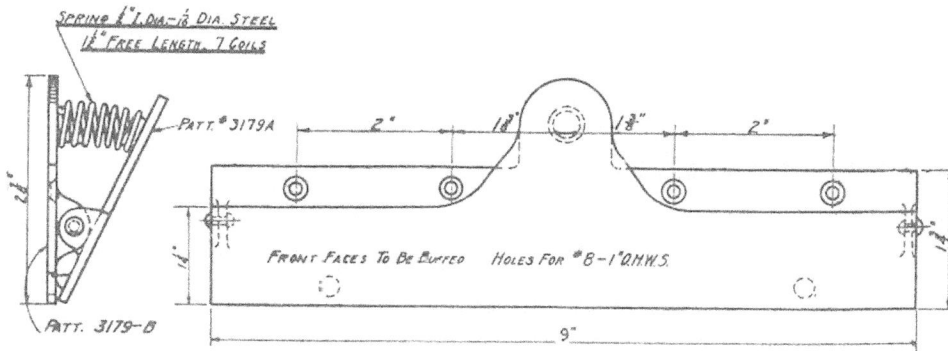

ADVERTISING CARD HOLDER (INSIDE)
No. 3179
BRONZE

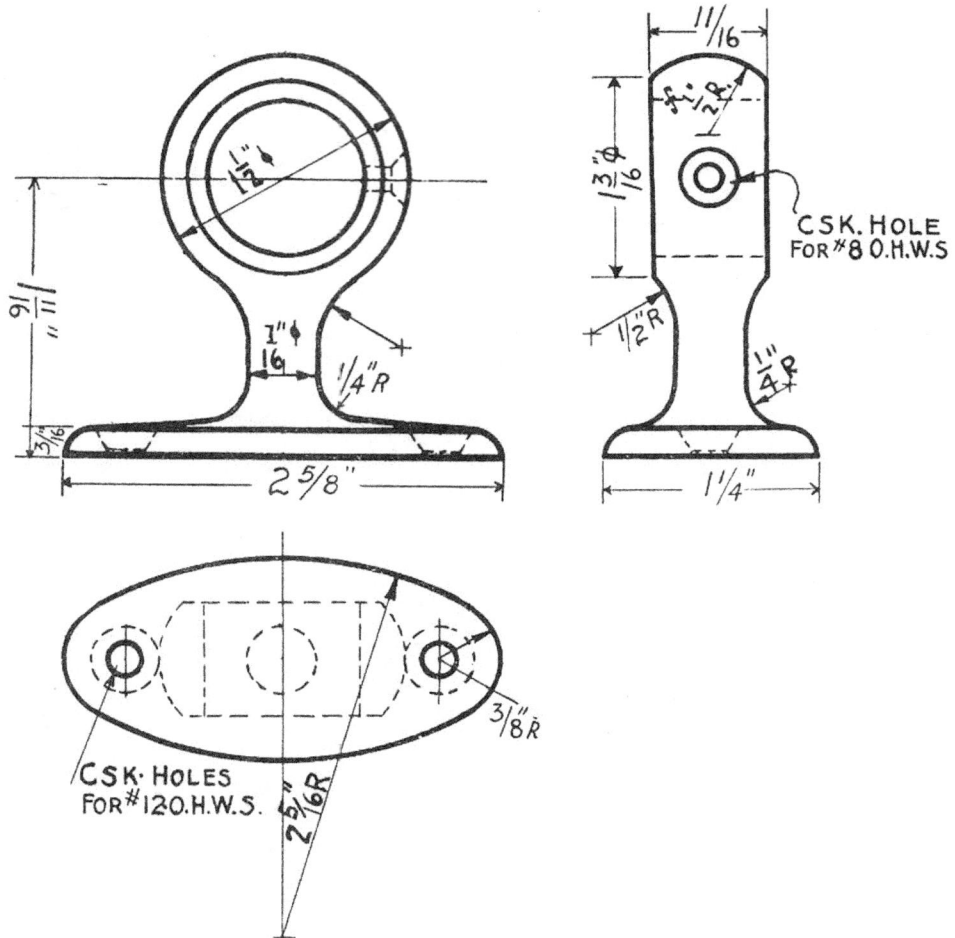

GRAB RAIL SOCKET
STREET CAR BUS
No. 3275
BRASS

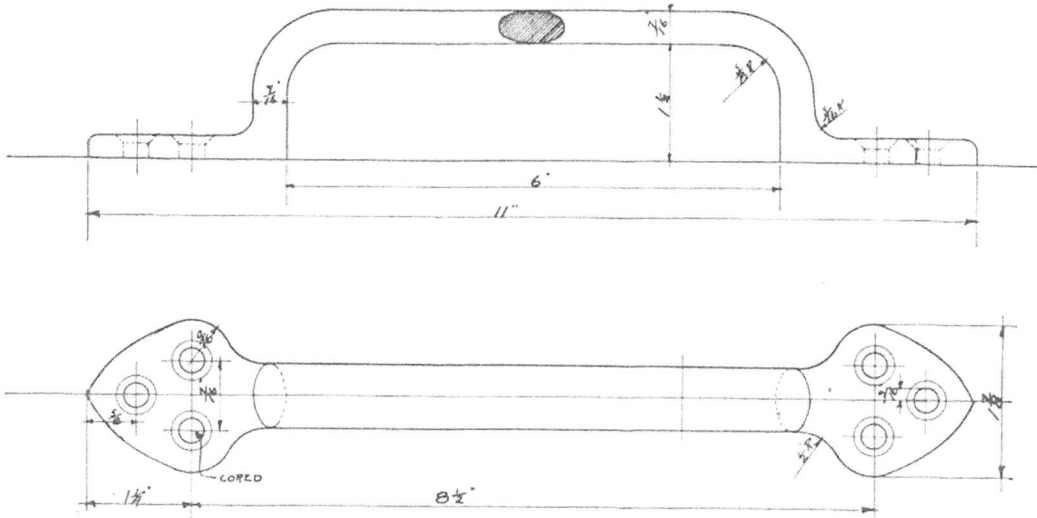

BIRNEY SAFETY CAR ROOF HANDLE
No. 404
MALLEABLE IRON

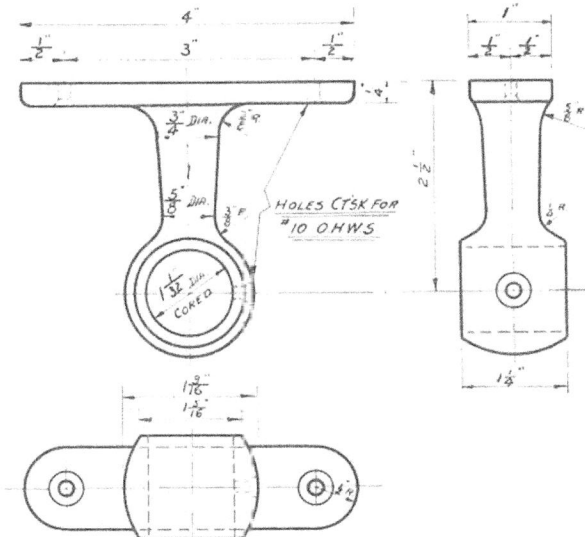

GRAB RAIL SOCKET
No 3161

BUS GRAB RAIL SOCKET
No. 3161
BRONZE, ALUMINUM OR MALLEABLE IRON

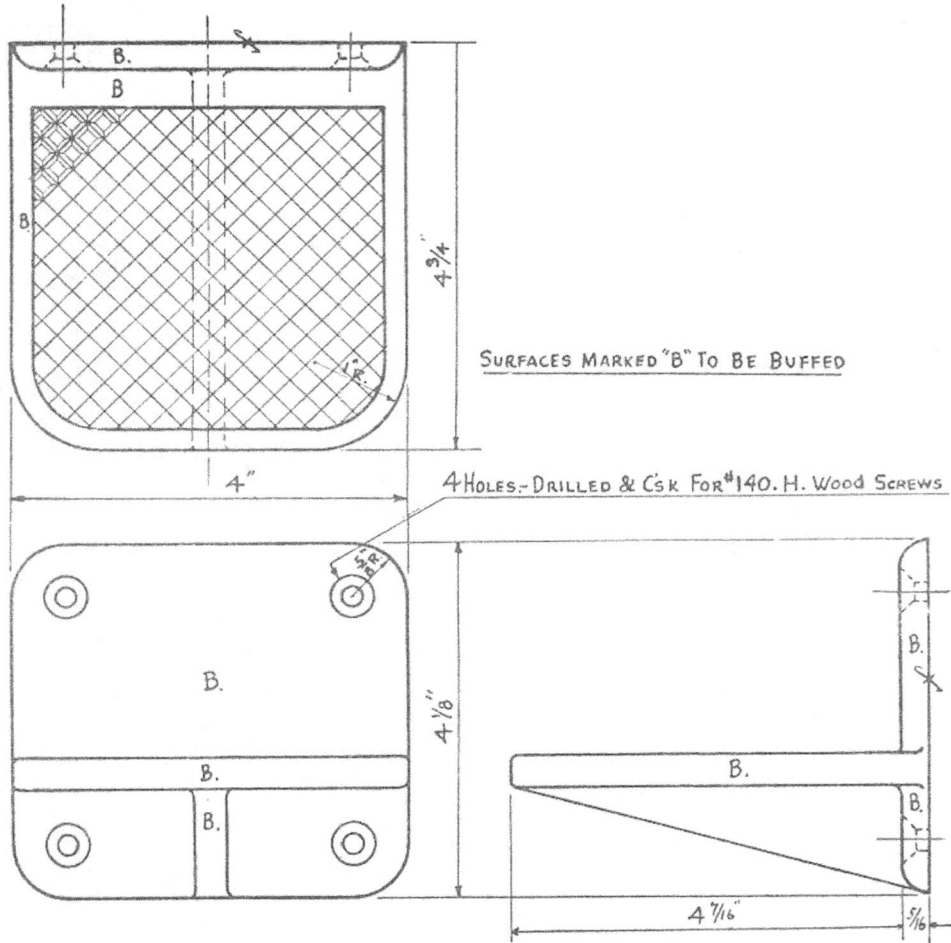

SURFACES MARKED "B" TO BE BUFFED

4 HOLES - DRILLED & C'sk FOR #140. H. WOOD SCREWS

4¾

4"

4⅛"

4 7/16"

5/16"

REAR STEP
21 PASSENGER CHAIR COACH
No. 3278
ALUMINUM

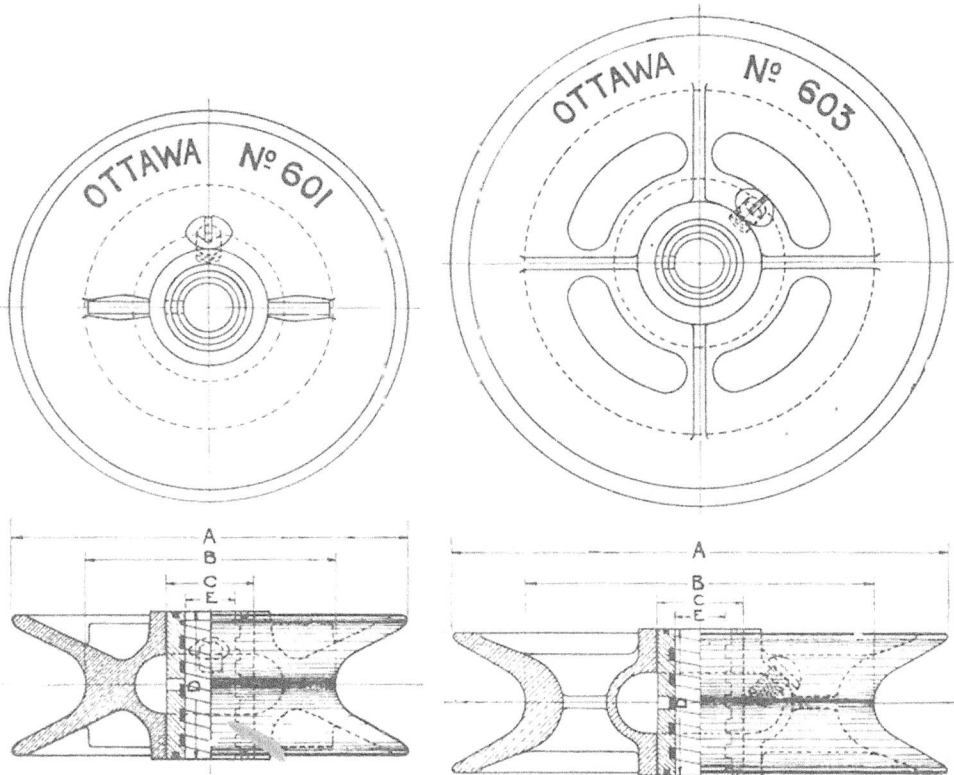

"OTTAWA" TROLLEY WHEEL

Name	Number	A	B	C	D	E*		Remarks
Ottawa	601	4"	2½"	⅞"	1½"	½"		Solid.
"	602	4½"	3"	⅞"	1½"	½"		Arms
								Weight 2 lbs. 0 oz. with bushing
"	603	5"	3¼"	⅞"	1½"	½"		Arms
"	604	5½"	3¾"	⅞"	1½"	½"		Arms
"	605	6"	4¼"	⅞"	1½"	½"		Arms

* Note — ⅝" Bushing can also be used with these wheels.

COMMERFORD SASH UPPER BEARING
No 3288

← A

SECTION A-A

B

B

A

COMMERFORD SASH LOWER BEARING AND LOCK
No. 3287

SECTION B-B

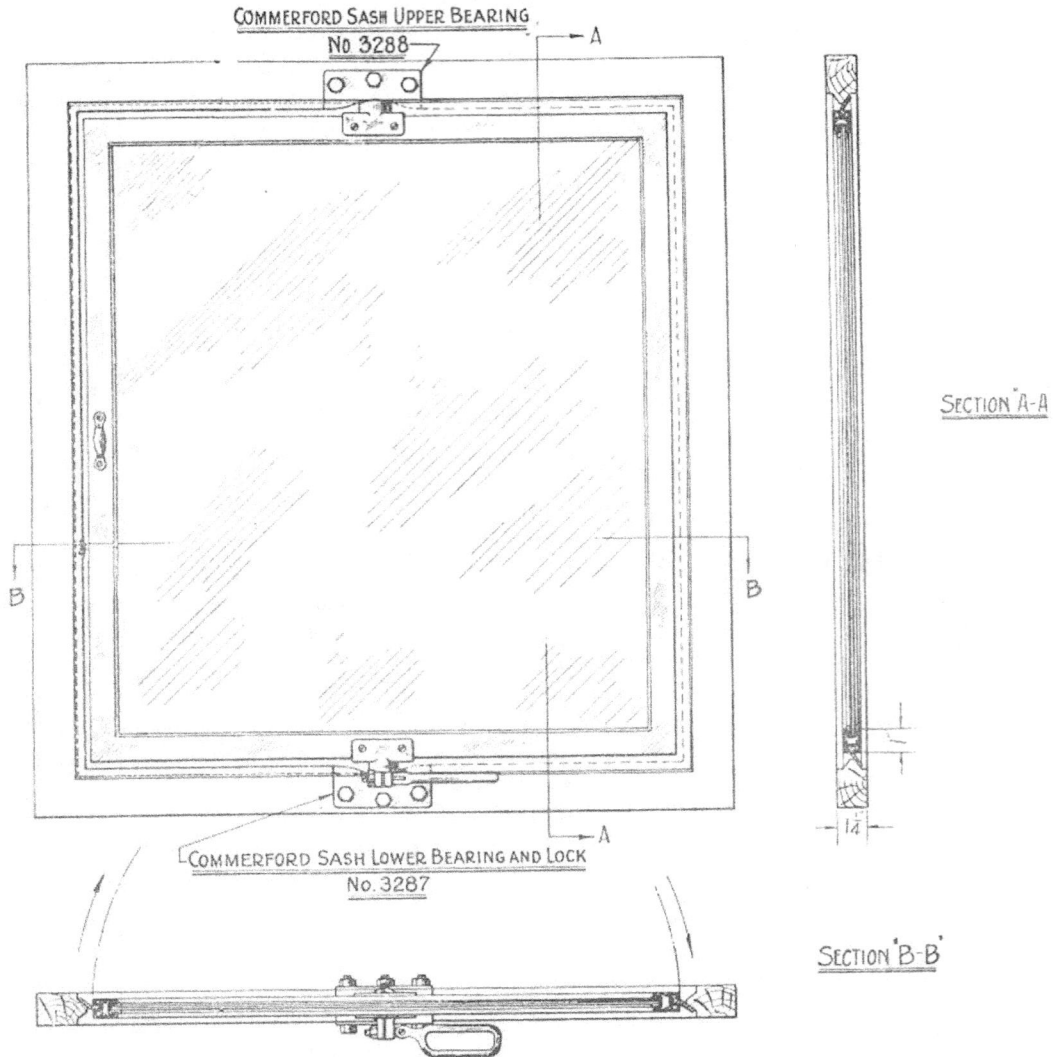

COMMERFORD MOTORMAN'S ALL-WEATHER SASH
(See page 95 for photograph)

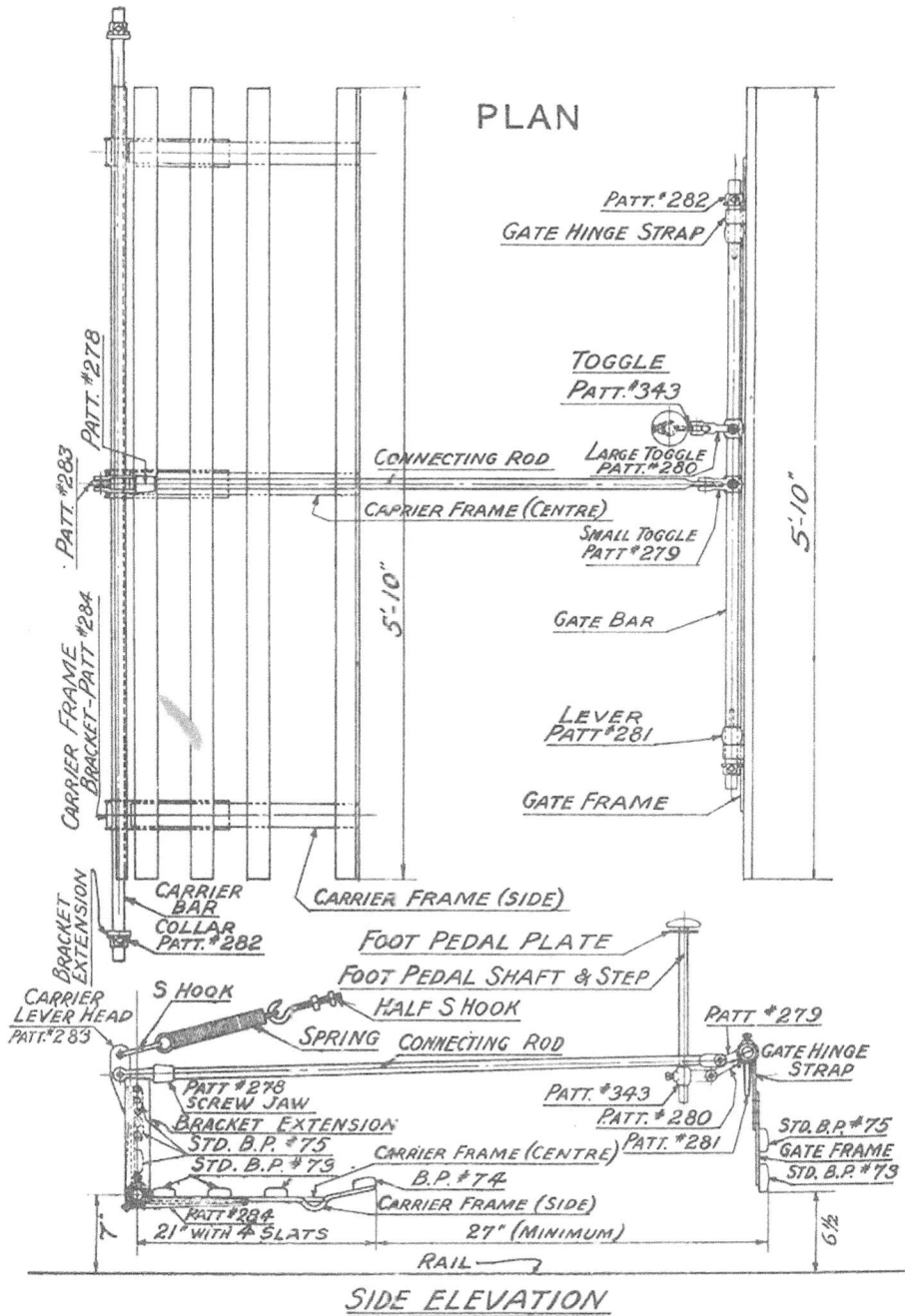

PLAN

PATT. #282
GATE HINGE STRAP

TOGGLE
PATT. #343

LARGE TOGGLE
PATT. #280

PATT. #278

PATT. #283

CONNECTING ROD

CARRIER FRAME (CENTRE)

SMALL TOGGLE
PATT #279

CARRIER FRAME #284
BRACKET-PATT #284

5'-10"

5'-10"

GATE BAR

LEVER
PATT #281

GATE FRAME

BRACKET EXTENSION

CARRIER BAR
COLLAR PATT. #282

CARRIER FRAME (SIDE)

CARRIER LEVER HEAD
PATT. #283

S HOOK

HALF S HOOK

FOOT PEDAL PLATE

FOOT PEDAL SHAFT & STEP

PATT #279

SPRING   CONNECTING ROD

GATE HINGE STRAP

PATT #278
SCREW JAW

BRACKET EXTENSION

STD. B.P. #75

STD. B.P. #73

PATT #343

PATT #280

PATT #281

CARRIER FRAME (CENTRE)

B.P. #74

CARRIER FRAME (SIDE)

STD. B.P. #75

GATE FRAME

STD. B.P. #73

PATT #284

21" WITH 4 SLATS

27" (MINIMUM)

6½

RAIL

SIDE ELEVATION

LIFE GUARD
O. C. Co.

4½ dia. of Cover

1⁵⁄₁₀" R

Drill & csk. for ¼" Scs.

Patt # 1978-A

Drill for ¼" bolt

4⅝

2½

2¾

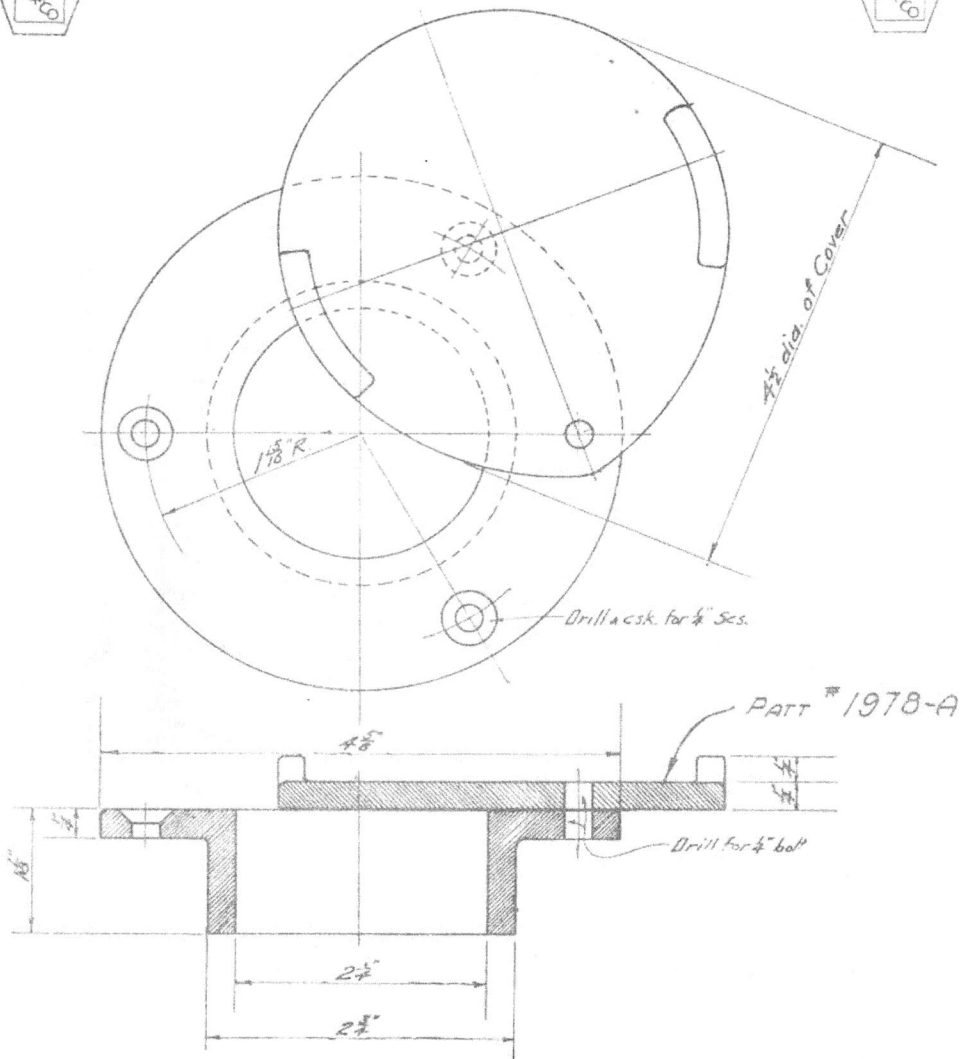

SWITCH BAR FLOOR FLANGE & COVER
Patt No. 1978-B
GREY IRON

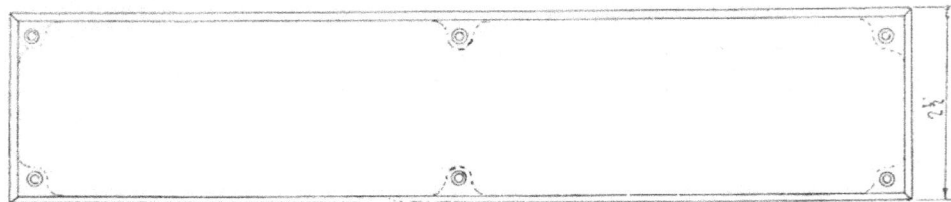

PUSH OR FINGER PLATE
No. 2628
BRONZE OR ALUMINUM

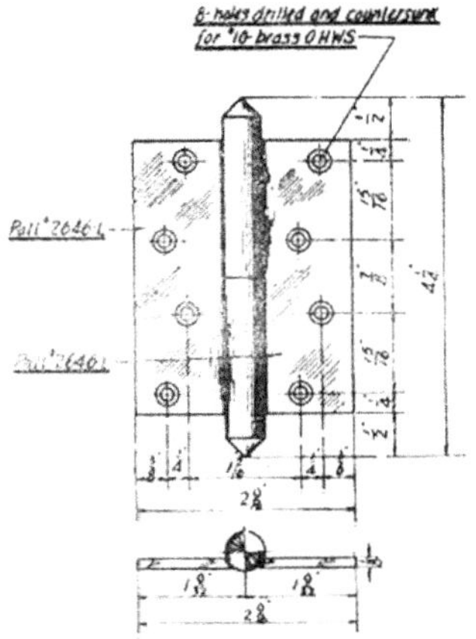

LOOSE JOINT BUTT HINGE
No. 2646 R. and L.
BRONZE

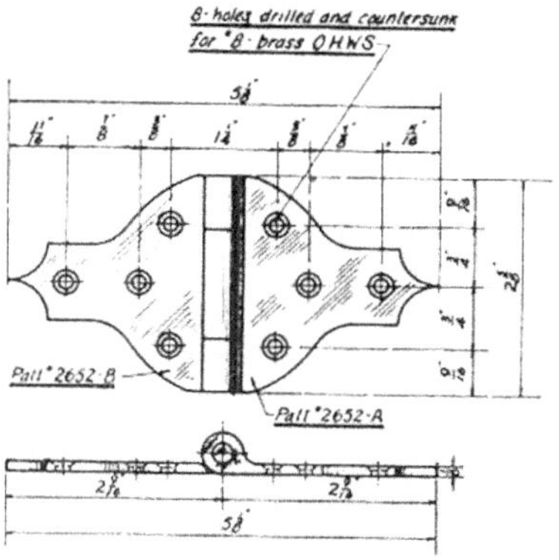

VESTIBULE DOOR STRAP
HINGE
No. 2652
BRONZE

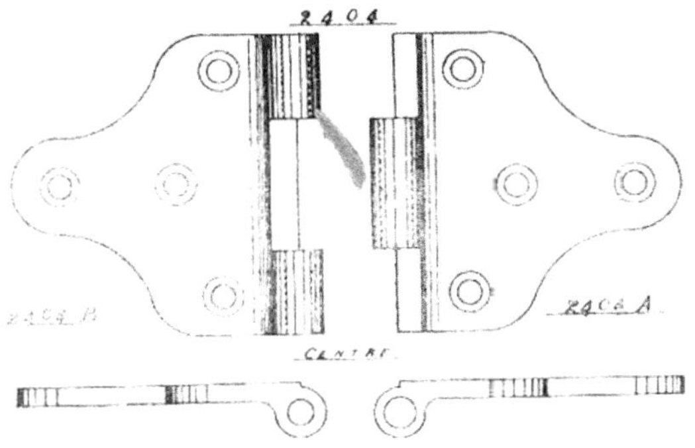

AUTOMATIC DOOR HINGE
SINGLE DOUBLE
No. 2404
BRONZE

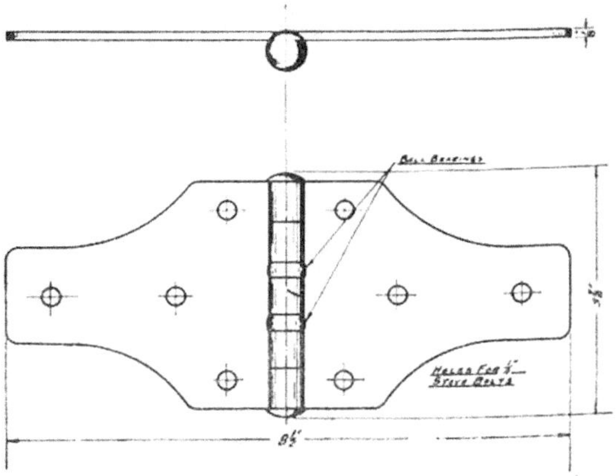

STANDARD BALL BEARING
HINGE
STEEL

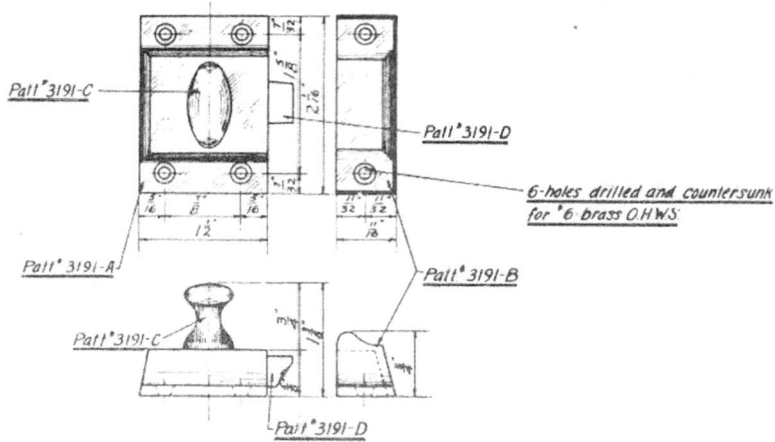

CUPBOARD CATCH
No. 3191
BRONZE

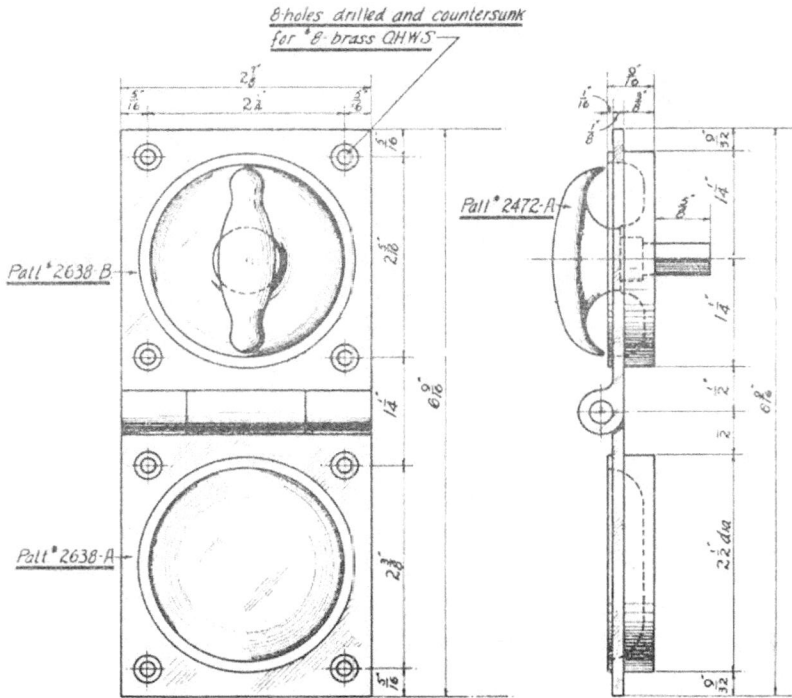

DOOR FLUSH HANDLE AND HINGE
No 2638
BRONZE

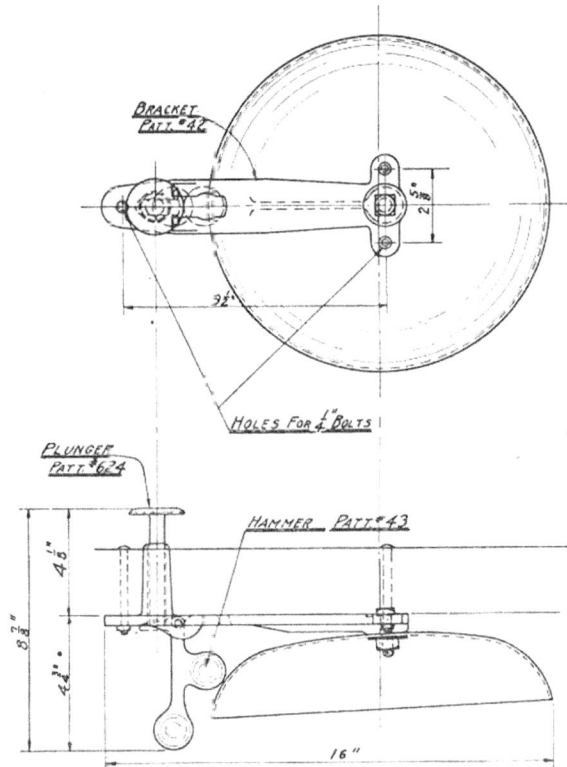

STANDARD 12 INCH GONG
No. 42

SHELL IS MADE OF STEEL. OTHER PARTS ARE MALLEABLE IRON.

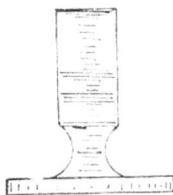

No. 2413   **DOOR HOLD BACK SETS**   No. 2909
BRONZE

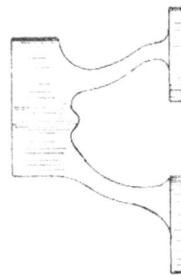

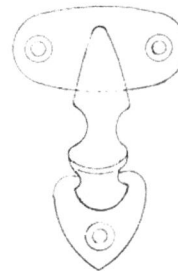

2425.A FRAME

10-OVALL HEAD WOOD SCREWS

2425.C HAMMER

2425.B BELL

2425.D HANGER

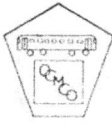

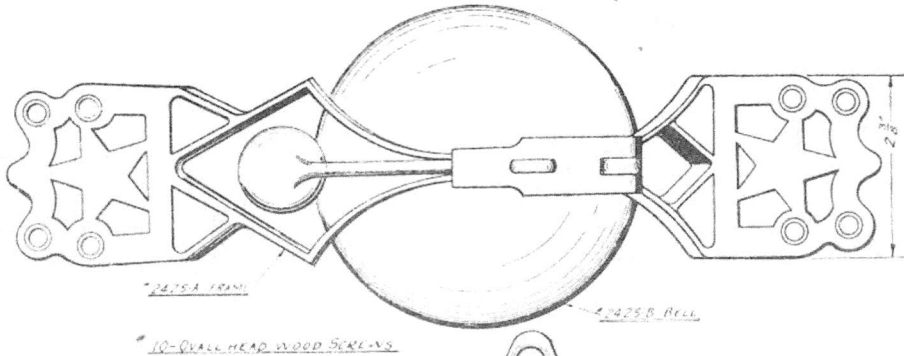

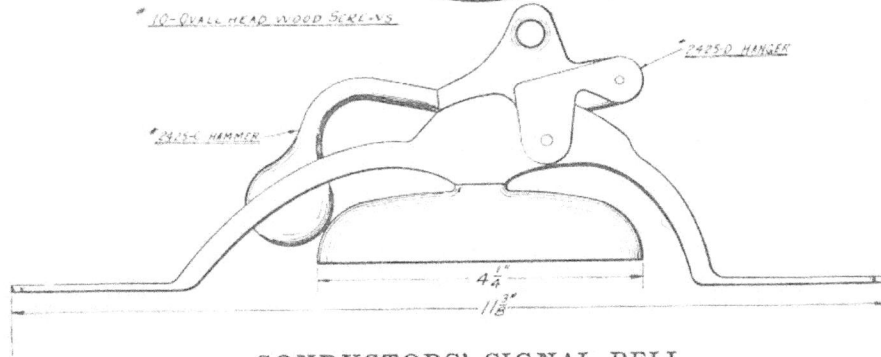

CONDUCTORS' SIGNAL BELL
No. 2425
BRONZE

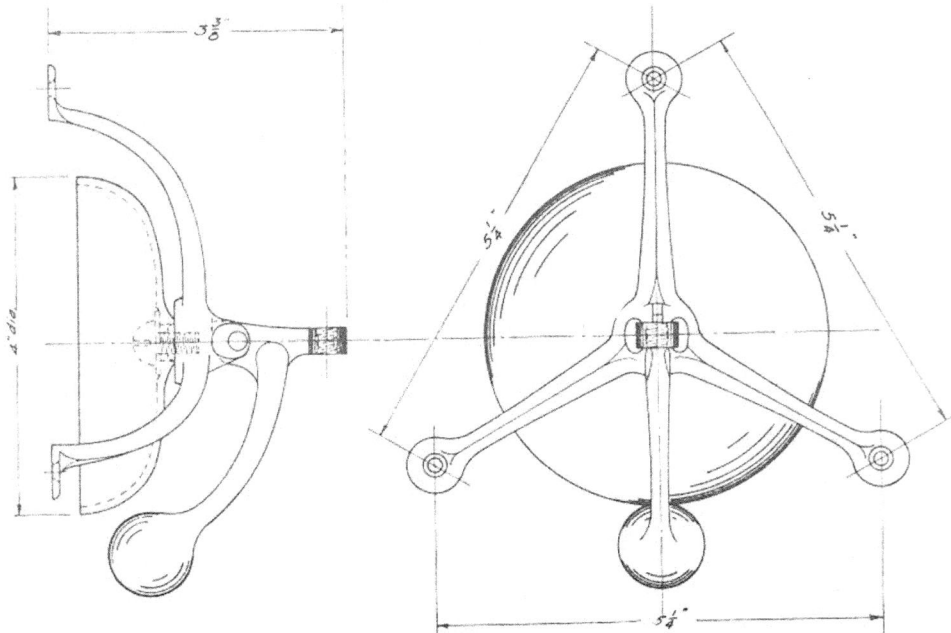

CONDUCTORS' SIGNAL BELL
No. 3102
BRONZE

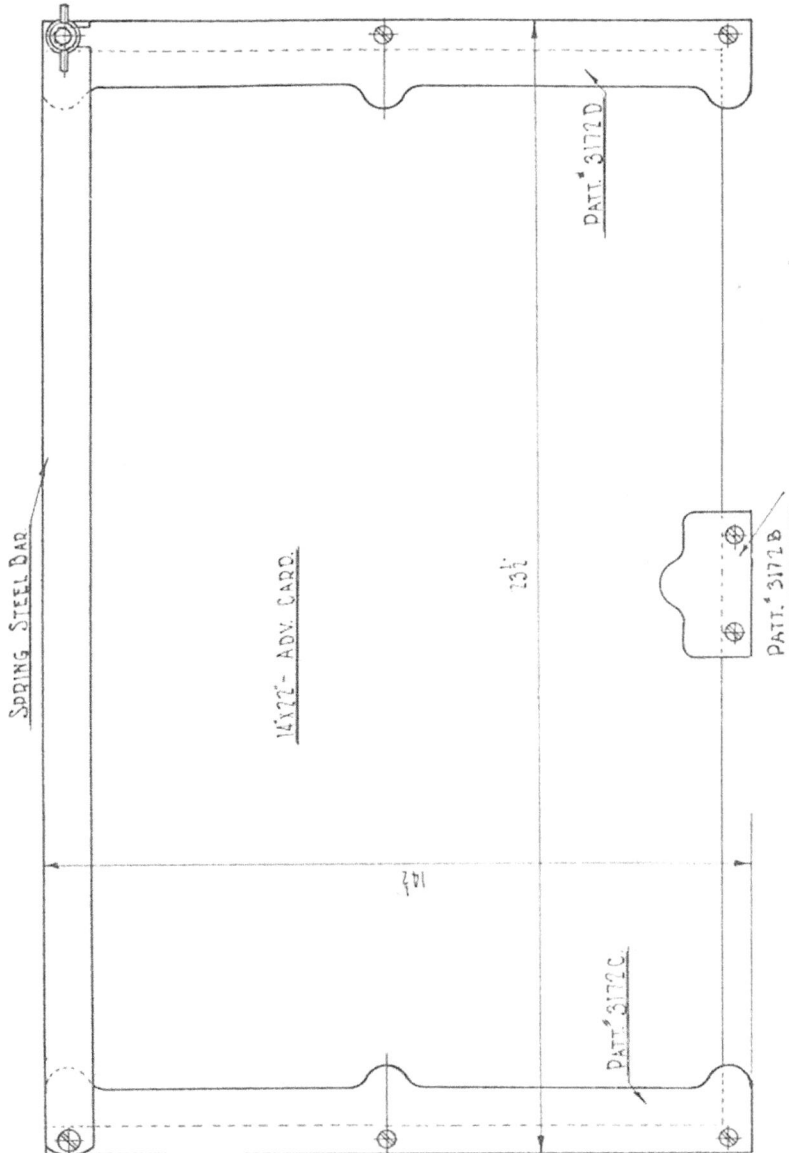

CARD HOLDER
No. 3172
BRONZE, ALUMINUM OR MALLEABLE IRON

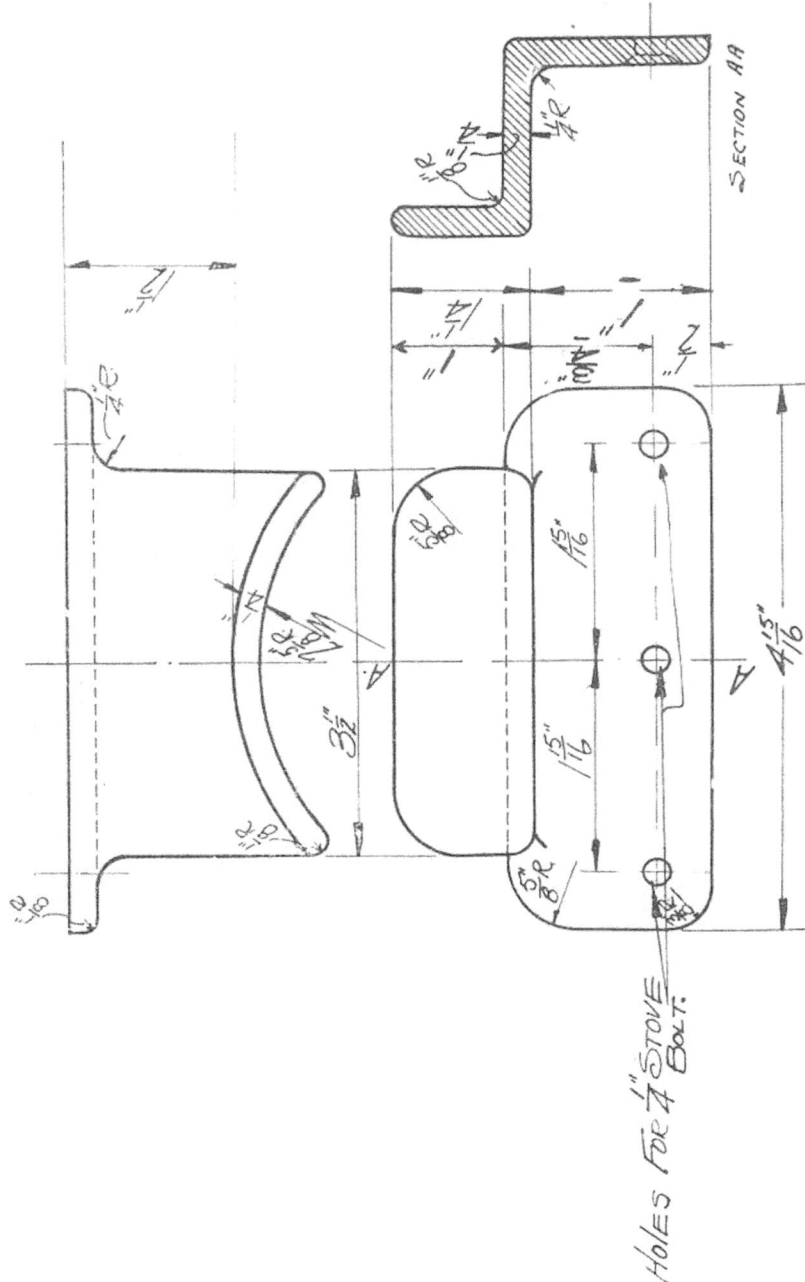

DOOR SHOE FOR BOTTOM OF DOOR
No. 3180
MALLEABLE IRON

AS REQUIRED

AS REQUIRED

288 C

$\frac{1"}{4}$ – IRON PIPE

288 A

288 B

$15\frac{9}{16}$

3"

288 D

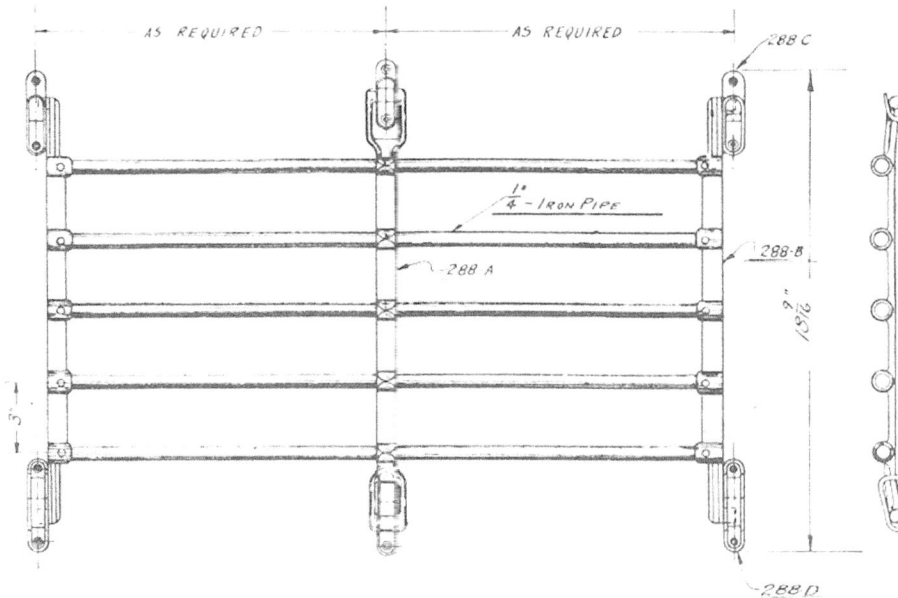

HINGED WINDOW GUARD
No. 288
BRACKETS — MALLEABLE IRON CASTINGS
RAILS — $\frac{1}{4}$" IRON PIPE

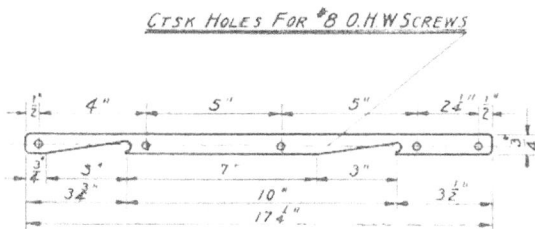

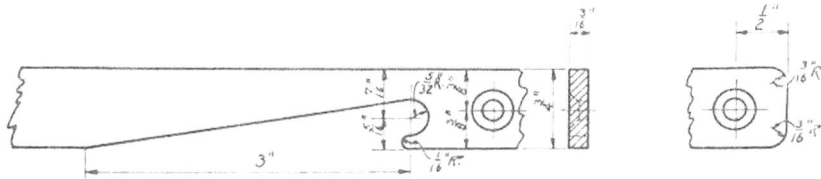

CTSK HOLES FOR #8 O.H.W SCREWS

$\frac{1}{2}$" 4" 5" 5" $2\frac{1}{2}$" $\frac{1}{2}$" $\frac{1}{2}$"

$\frac{3}{4}$"

$\frac{3}{4}$" 3" 7" 3" $3\frac{1}{2}$"

$3\frac{3}{4}$"

10"

$17\frac{1}{4}$"

$\frac{3}{16}$"

$\frac{1}{2}$"

$\frac{3}{16}$ R

3"

DROP SASH STOP BAR
No. 3251
BRONZE

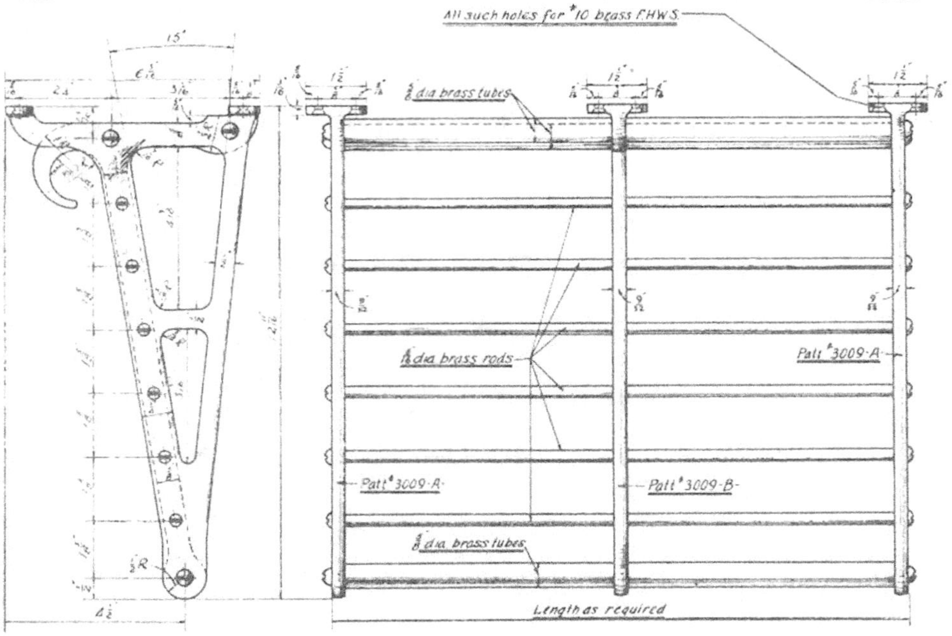

All such holes for #10 brass F.H.W.S.

Patt #3009·A

Patt #3009·A   Patt #3009·B

PARCEL RACK
No. 3009
BRONZE.

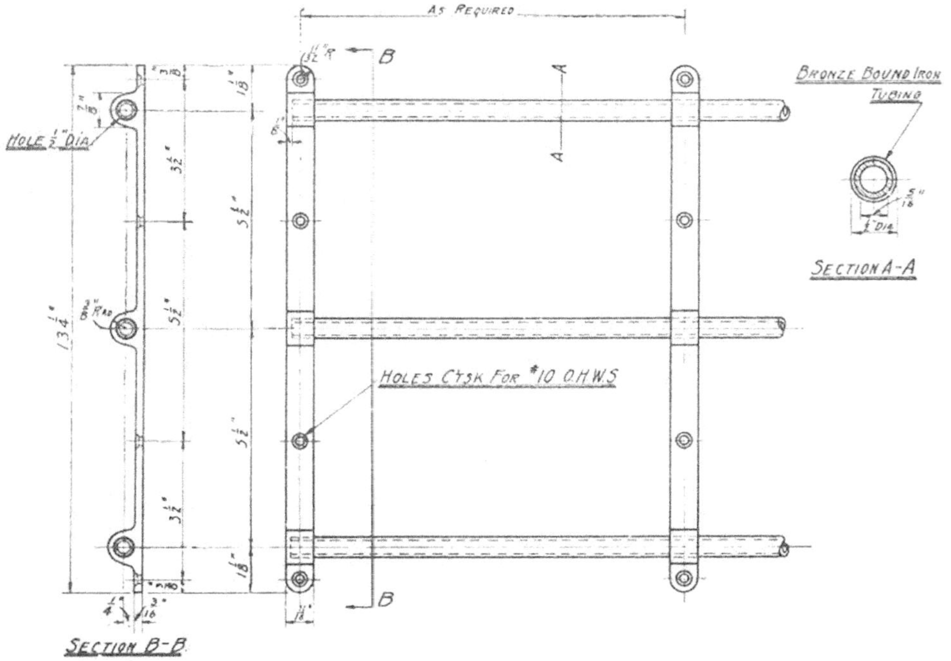

AS REQUIRED

BRONZE BOUND IRON
TUBING

SECTION A-A

HOLES CTSK FOR #10 O.H.W.S

SECTION B-B

WINDOW GUARD
No. 3129
BRONZE, ALUMINUM OR MALLEABLE IRON

HOLES FOR #9. O.H.W.S.

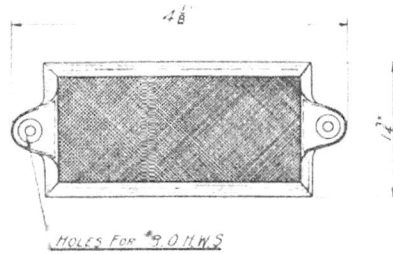

MATCH SCRATCH
No. 2496
BRONZE

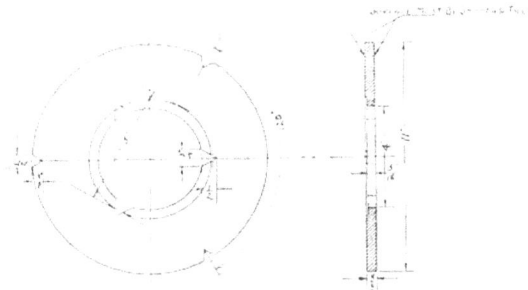

S.O. 1206

CENTRE PLATE RING
No. 3116
BRONZE

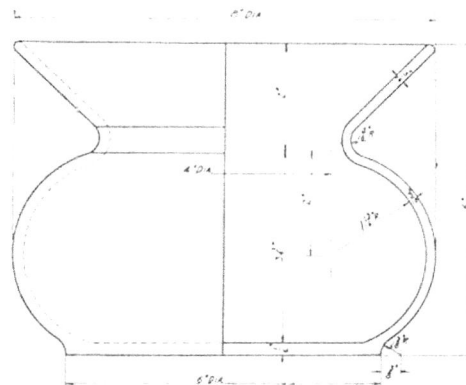

CUSPIDOR
No. 3190
BRONZE

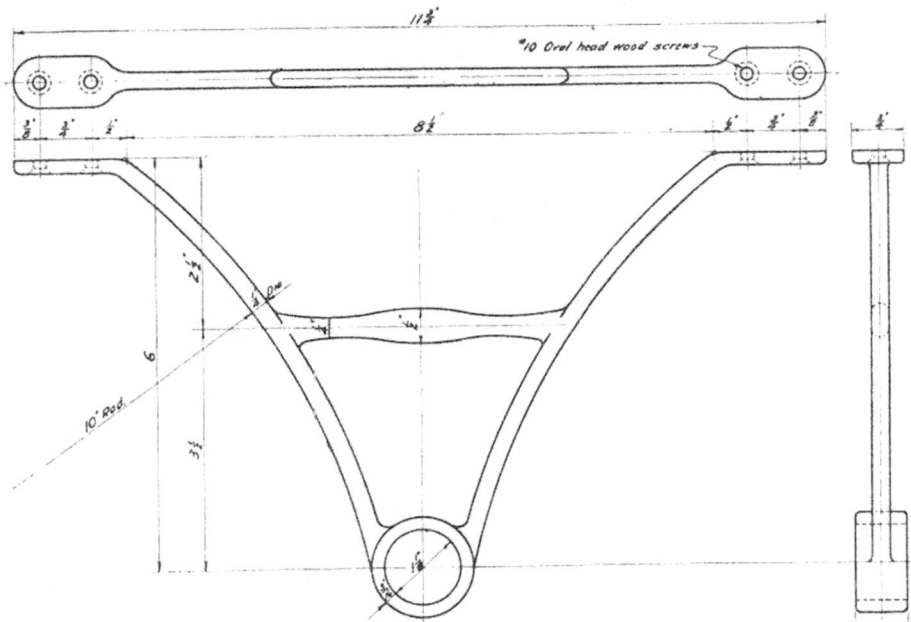

HAND POLE BRACKET.
BRONZE.
PATTERN Nº 3047.

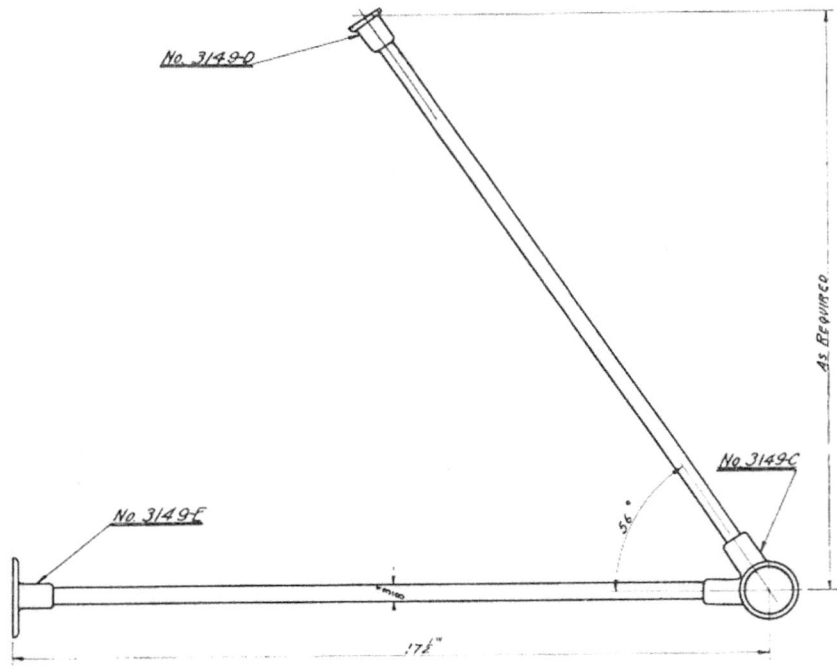

No. 3149-D

No. 3149C

No. 3149-F

56°

17½"

GRAB RAIL BRACKET
BRONZE

#2640

#2640

1#2640 A. Bolt or Keeper
1#2640 B. Bolt
1#2640 C. Case

#2639

Weight 1 lb. 1 oz.

Weight 2 lbs. 2 ozs.

BRONZE

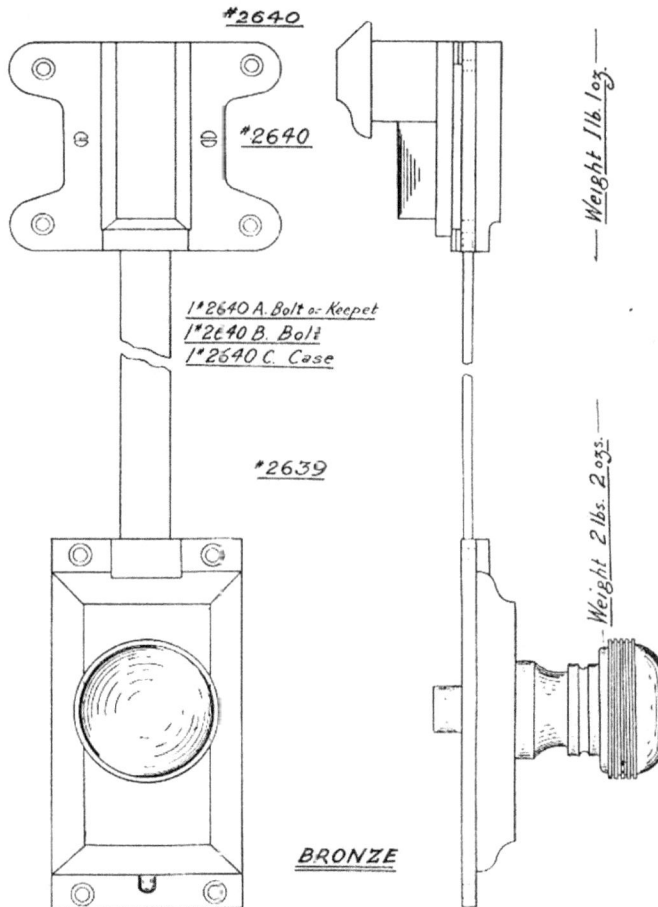

VESTIBULE AUTOMATIC DOOR LOCK
Spring Case and Knob
No. 2640
Bronze

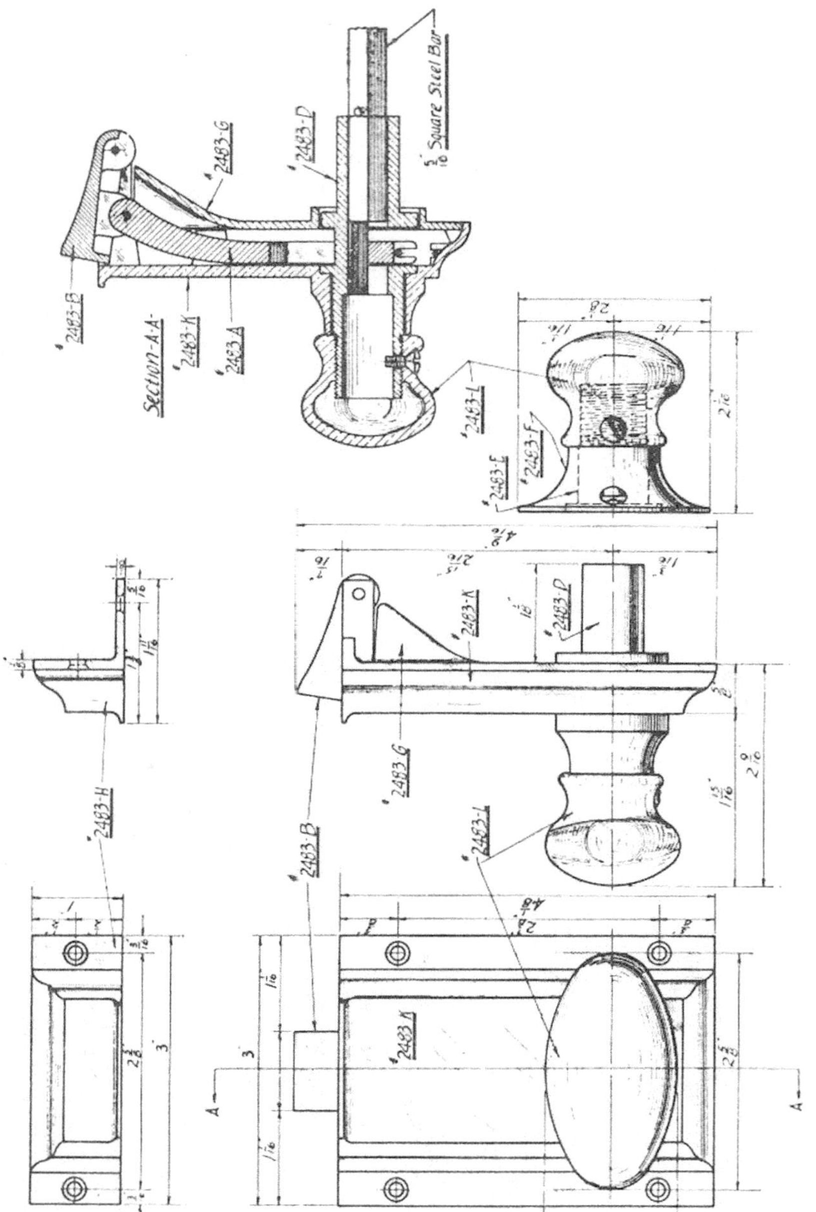

DOOR LOCK
No. 2483
BRONZE

HOLES FOR #8 O.H.SCREWS

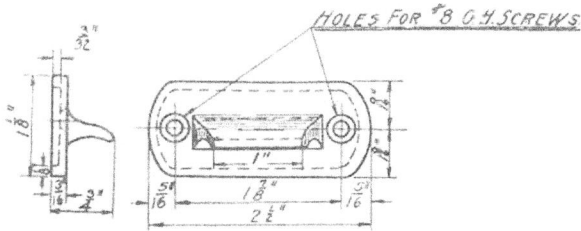

SASH LIFT
No. 3124
BRONZE OR ALUMINUM

COAT HOOK
No. 3126
BRONZE

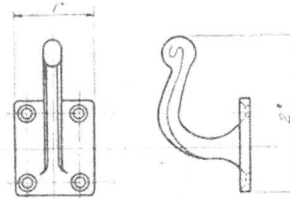

HOLES FOR #6 WOOD SCREWS

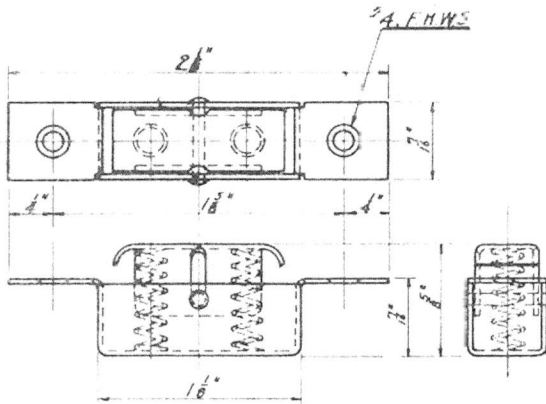

SASH ANTI-RATTLER
PLUNGER TYPE
BRASS
No. B-1029

SASH ANTI-RATTLER
CAM. TYPE
BRASS
No. B-1030

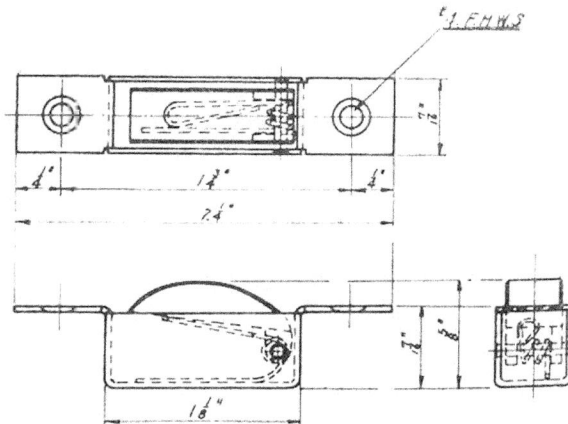

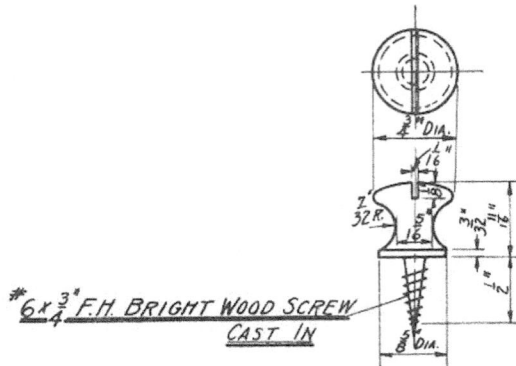

$\frac{3}{4}$" DIA.

$\frac{1}{16}$"

$\frac{7}{32}$ R.

$\frac{5}{16}$

$\frac{3}{32}$"

$\frac{11}{16}$"

$\frac{1}{2}$"

$\frac{3}{8}$ DIA.

#6 x $\frac{3}{4}$" F.H. BRIGHT WOOD SCREW
CAST IN

BRASS SCREW KNOB
No. 3127
BRONZE

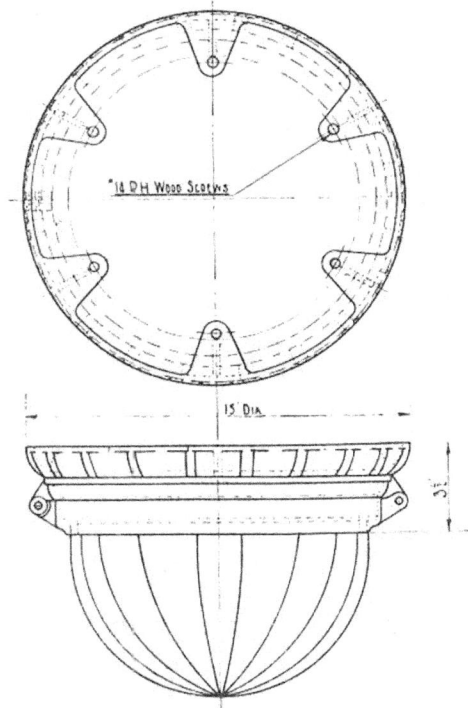

14 R.H. WOOD SCREWS

15 DIA.

DOME LIGHT
No. 3188
BRONZE

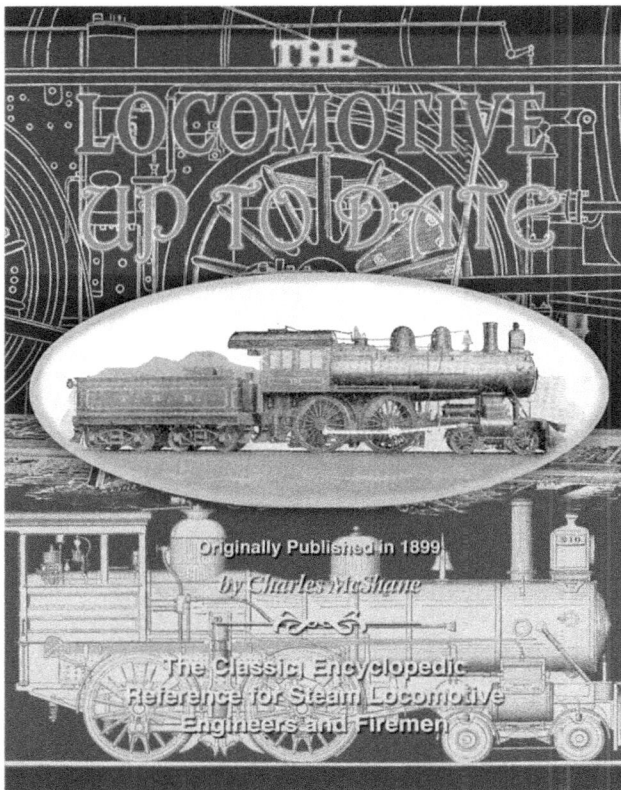
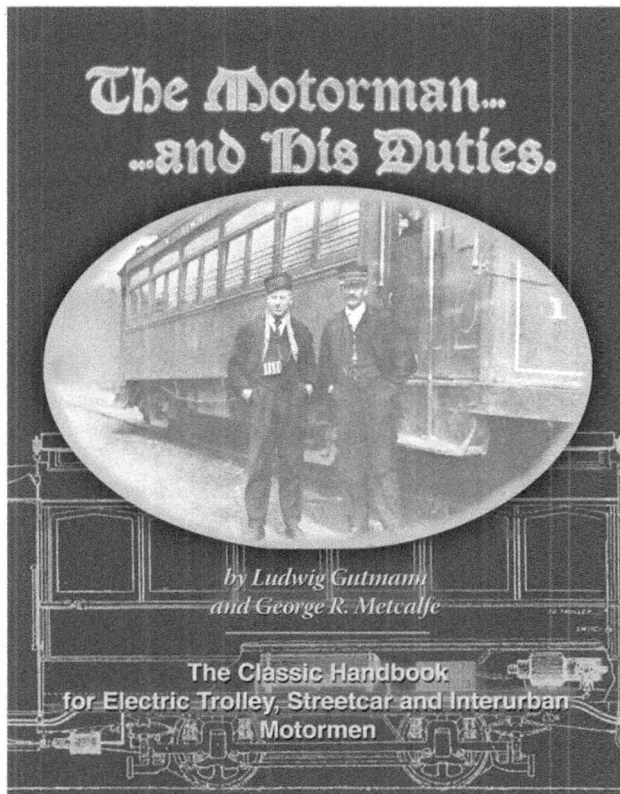

THE CLASSIC 1911 TROLLEY CAR
BUILDER'S REFERENCE BOOK

ELECTRIC
RAILWAY
DICTIONARY

By Rodney Hitt
Associate Editor, Electric Railway Journal

REPRINTED BY PERISCOPEFILM.COM

THE CLASSIC 1915 TROLLEY CAR
AND INTERURBAN RAILWAY BOOK

ELECTRIC
RAILWAY
ENGINEERING

By Francis H. Doane, A.M.B.

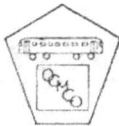

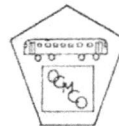

www.ingramcontent.com/pod-product-compliance
Lightning Source LLC
LaVergne TN
LVHW081324060426
835511LV00011B/1849